CAIRO PAPERS IN SOCIAL SCIENCE
VOLUME 34 NUMBER 4

The Food Question in the Middle East

Edited by
Malak S. Rouchdy
Iman A. Hamdy

Contributors
Habib Ayeb Hala N. Barakat
Ellis Goldberg Christian Henderson
Khaled Mansour Saker El Nour
Sara Pozzi Sara El Sayed

THE AMERICAN UNIVERSITY IN CAIRO PRESS
CAIRO NEW YORK

Cover photo: *shamsi* bread courtesy of Nassef Azmi

This paperback edition first published in 2023 by
The American University in Cairo Press
113 Sharia Kasr el Aini, Cairo, Egypt
420 Lexington Avenue, Suite 1644, New York, NY 10170
www.aucpress.com

First published in an electronic edition in 2017

Copyright © 2017, 2023 by the American University in Cairo Press

All rights reserved. No part of this publication may be reproduced, stored in a retrieval system, or transmitted in any form or by any means, electronic, mechanical, photocopying, recording, or otherwise, without the prior written permission of the publisher.

ISBN 978 1 649 03234 8

Names: Rouchdy, Malak, editor. | Ḥamdī, Īmān, editor. | Ayeb, Habib, author.
Title: The food question in the Middle East / edited by Malak S. Rouchdy, Iman A. Hamdy ; contributors, Habib Ayeb [and 7 others].
Identifiers: LCCN 2022016231 | ISBN 9781649032348 (paperback) | ISBN 9781617978562 (epub) | ISBN 9781617978098 (adobe pdf)
Subjects: LCSH: Food supply--Middle East. | Food supply--Political aspects--Middle East. | Food security--Middle East.
Classification: LCC HD9016.N32 F66 2022 | DDC 363.80956--dc23/eng/20220511

1 2 3 4 5   27 26 25 24 23

Designed by Adam el-Sehemy

Contents

1	Introduction *Malak S. Rouchdy and Iman A. Hamdy*	1
2	We Are What We Eat, We Were What We Ate *Hala N. Barakat*	7
3	Killing Them Softly: Dietary Deficiencies and Food Insecurity in Twentieth-Century Egypt *Ellis Goldberg*	25
4	Where is Our *Baladi* Food? *Sara Pozzi and Sara El Sayed*	47
5	Agri-food System Dynamics in a South Lebanon Village, 1920–2015 *Saker El Nour*	63
6	Food Issues and Revolution: The Process of Dispossession, Class Solidarity, and Popular Uprising: The Case of Sidi Bouzid in Tunisia *Habib Ayeb*	89
7	Reflection on the Concept of Hunger: The Case of Egypt between 2008 and 2011 *Malak S. Rouchdy*	115

8 Gulf Land Acquisitions in Egypt and Sudan:
   Food Security or the Agro-commodity Supply Chain?   131
   Christian Henderson

9 Politics of Food Aid: From Politicization to Integration   145
   Khaled Mansour

   About the Contributors   173

CHAPTER 1

Introduction

Malak S. Rouchdy and Iman A. Hamdy

In recent years, the food question has been a central concern for politicians, economists, international organizations, activists, and NGOs alike, as well as social scientists at large. Even though this is not a new phenomenon, two main factors contributed to the centrality of food questions in the first decade of the twenty-first century: 1) the global food crisis and its impact on the environment, and the political economy and security of the global South; 2) the expansion of scholarly studies relating food issues to agrarian questions with the objective of developing theoretical frameworks that would allow for a critical analysis of the current food issues at the historical, cultural, social, political, and economic levels.

Today, social sciences are offering important contributions along these lines. By first taking the analysis of food and agrarian questions beyond the gates of the farm, by locating it within the wider political economy system both regionally and globally, and, second, by approaching it as a whole system in which the farmer (producer) as well as the consumer become central actors as well as market agents and state agents, a more comprehensive and multilayered analysis is proposed. The works of Harriet Friedmann (2009; 2005; Friedmann and McMichael 1989) and Philip McMichael (2009; 2005; 2004; 1987) as well as Campbell (2009) are foundational in the introduction and the development of the food regime approach. This approach examines closely the institutions and the agents behind the restructuring of the social, cultural, and political relations in the food system. According to this approach, food regime could be understood as the analysis of the political, economic, and social organization of food in a given society at various historical periods. The food regime approach is historically delineated; it is regionally specific and culturally relative to the history and geography in which it is situated. While it rejects the linearity underpinning modernization and development theories, it invokes instead multiple theoretical frameworks such as structuralism, agency, and contingency theories, to analyze the dynamic and conflicting relationships that prevail in the food chain. Food regime is an approach and not a conceptual framework; its vision is based on the assumption that there is no predetermined development of the food system; therefore, it implies that food systems are to be traced in the economy, in politics, in culture, and in society at large. By approaching the food system beyond the gates of the farm, and examining it above and below the confinement of the nation-state, it offers a wide theoretical potential for the analysis of the fluidity and the complexity of the food system at a given time, in given places, and among particular groups. As such, it goes beyond the nation-state to include many analytical concepts, such as agency, organization/institution, legitimacy, technology, scarcity, precariousness, abundance, and so on. Perhaps the main contribution of this approach is that it opens the doors for the analysis of the structural, the legal, the political, the cultural, and the subjective dimensions of the food systems. It is within such an approach that the act of eating, for example, could be analytically viewed as socially, culturally, economically, and politically grounded (Warde 1997; Ferrières 2002, 2007; Ariès 1997; Ascher 2005; Fischler 2013).

Adopting the food regime approach, the following chapters will address the production process and political economy aspects of food, while focusing on the following aspects:

1) The role of technology and culture in the historical development of food practices.
2) The role of states, markets, and international food agencies in shaping national food politics.
3) The changing local political dynamics under food systems.
4) Emerging sociopolitical trends in establishing alternative agricultural and food practices.

Critical Themes Related to the Food Question

The second chapter in this volume, written by Hala Barakat, argues against the traditional concept of food heritage. In her overview of food production since prehistoric times, Barakat traces the introduction of new plants and spices in Egypt in different eras that with time became part of the food heritage. For her, what we call "national cuisine" is always changing, appropriating new crops and foods and integrating them into the local culture.

Ellis Goldberg also alludes to the transmission of crops across the globe. However, crops have a life of their own. Here, the issue is not only about eating but the techniques used in processing and consuming food. That is why certain crops may have adverse effects on human health if not handled properly in their new environment. Goldberg makes his case by recounting how the dependence on maize as the main grain in rural Egypt from the nineteenth to the mid twentieth century was associated with the spread of pellagra, although it has been the dominant crop in the New World for thousands of years without doing any harm. The reason behind this lies in the fact that the Europeans brought in maize from the New World to the Old World without adopting the food technology that went with it in the New World.

While Hala Barakat challenges the idea of authentic food, Sara Pozzi and Sara El Sayed believe in the idea of food heritage. They seek to valorize local food products, not only at the theoretical but the practical level as well, in order to enhance local food sovereignty and safeguard the Egyptian sociocultural and environmental ecosystems. Their chapter is an account of the Baladini project, which they initiated in a rural community in Giza governorate with the aim of encouraging rural women to produce and sell traditional food products using local components and ingredients.

In chapter five, Saker El Nour shifts the scene to Lebanon, where he traces the development of the agri-food system in Sinay, a village in South Lebanon, from 1920 to 2015, claiming that it has passed through four distinct phases. The shift from one stage to another corresponds to changes in national policies and global food regime dynamics. At present, the village food-diet system is dominated by two opposing trends, a westernized system of meat and industrialized products and a localized system based on local agricultural and natural products.

While the previous chapters dealt with food systems, the next two will focus on how national neoliberal agricultural policies in Tunisia and Egypt led to the impoverishment of large segments of the population, especially in rural areas, and how this in turn led to political discontent and popular upheavals against the ruling regimes. In the chapter on Tunisia, Habib Ayeb shows how the suicide of Bouazizi, which triggered the revolution against Ben Ali, was more than an individual act by an unemployed university graduate who was humiliated by a policewoman—the story that the regime and the media sought to present. Rather, it is the result of a decades-long systematic impoverishment of the Sidi Bouzid region, to which Bouazizi belonged, and the dispossession of its local farming communities at the hands of the government and big local and foreign investors. To quote Ayeb, "The unleashing of massive mobilization, beginning on December 17, 2010, can be explained in large part by a form of class solidarity on the part of the Sidi Bouzid peasantry in the face of the loss of one of their own."

In Egypt, Malak Rouchdy shows how comparable economic policies and the global food crisis in 2008 led to widespread fears among Egyptian policymakers and the media of the eruption of a revolt of the hungry if the economic situation failed to improve. Focusing on the government reaction to this crisis, Rouchdy shows how the regime attempted to defuse public anger by justifying its policies and constructing a discourse that depoliticized the concept of 'hunger' in collaboration with international organizations and corporate institutions. The case of the Egyptian Food Bank, established in 2006, is an illustration of the claim by the elite that "hunger is not the outcome of a poor economic system but the result of a lack of social solidarity, morality, and religion," in Rouchdy's words. Through acts of charity, the Bank claimed as its mission the eradication of hunger by 2025 in collaboration with the state.

Not only does neoliberalism affect national politics, but it also casts its shadows at the regional level as well. This is what Christian Henderson argues in his chapter, which examines agricultural projects in Gulf-owned land in Egypt and Sudan. In the past two decades, investors from Gulf countries have been acquiring agricultural land in those two countries for cultivation purposes, especially in reclaimed areas. While they seek to justify these projects as a means to enhance food security in the Arab countries, these projects in fact exploit the land and water resources in Egypt and Sudan to produce crops that serve the needs of the agro-industrial conglomerates owned by Gulf capital without offering any benefit to the local populations.

Addressing another critical aspect of the food issue at the regional level, the last chapter, by Khaled Mansour, gives an account of the politicization of food aid to war-torn countries, focusing particularly on Syria and Iraq. Mansour, who at one point worked for the World Food Programme (WFP), gives the background of the creation of the WFP and shows how the process of seeking to provide food aid to needed areas in war zones compromises "the humanitarian principles of impartiality, neutrality, and independence." Aid officials end up coordinating with institutions, governments, militias, and local communities to set their priorities and have access to target areas, a process which entails a high degree of professionalization and bureaucratization. During this process, aid institutions themselves become self-conscious actors with their own interests to serve, including the well-being of the institution and its ability to face competition. These concerns lead them to adopt pragmatic policies that may conflict with humanitarian principles and cause more harm than good to the people they attempt to help.

References

Ariès, Paul. 1977. *La fin des mangeurs. Les métamorphoses de la table à l'âge de la modernisation alimentaire*. Paris: Desclée et Brouwer.

Ascher, François. 2005. *Le mangeur hypermoderne*. Paris: Odile Jacob.

Campbell, Hugh. 2009. "Breaking New Ground in Food Regime Theory: Corporate Environmentalism, Ecological Feedbacks and the 'Food from Somewhere' Regime?" *Agriculture and Human Values*, 26: 309–319.

Ferrières, Madeleine. 2002. *Histoires des peurs alimentaires. Du Moyen-Âge à l'aube du XXe siècle*. Paris: Éd. du Seuil, coll. L'univers historique.

———. 2007. *Nourritures canailles*. Paris: Éd. du Seuil, coll. L'univers historique.

Fischler, Claude. 2001. *L'Homnivore*. Paris: Odile Jacob.

Friedmann, Harriet. 2005. "From Colonialism to Green Capitalism: Social Movements and the Emergence of Food Regimes."

In Frederick H. Buttel and P. McMichael, eds., *New Directions in the Sociology of Global Development: Research in Rural Sociology and Development*, 11: 227–264. Amsterdam: Elsevier.

———. 2009. "Moving Food Regimes Forward: Reflections on Symposium Essays," *Agriculture and Human Values*, 26(4): 335–344.

Friedmann, Harriet, and Philip McMichael. 1989. "Agriculture and the State System: The Rise and Decline of National Agricultures, 1870 to Present," *Sociologia Ruralis*, 29(2): 93–117.

McMichael, Philip. 1987. "Bringing Circulation Back into Agricultural Political Economy: Analyzing the Antebellum Plantation in Its World Market Context," *Rural Sociology*, 52(2): 242–263.

———. 2004. *Development and Social Change: A Global Perspective*, 3rd ed. Thousand Oaks, CA: Pine Forge Press.

———. 2005. "Global Change and the Food Regime." In Frederick H. Buttel and Philip McMichael, eds., *New Directions in the Sociology of Global Development: Research in Rural Sociology and Development*, 11: 269–303. Amsterdam: Elsevier.

———. 2009. "A Food Regime Analysis of the 'World Food Crisis'," *Agriculture and Human Values*, 26: 281–295.

Warde, Alan. 1997. *Consumption, Food and Taste: Culinary Antinomies and Commodity Culture*. London: Sage Publications.

CHAPTER 2

We Are What We Eat, We Were What We Ate

Hala N. Barakat

Introduction

This chapter traces the beginnings of food production in Egypt since prehistoric times and follows its evolution through history. This journey explores the gradual introduction of plants and some animals to Egypt for consumption and discusses how and why these species have become part of the 'Egyptian food heritage' as it is known today. The chapter also challenges the traditional concept of food heritage in relation to local, regional, and global events and how these have affected food practices all over the world, and particularly in Egypt, over the millennia.

The Prehistoric Era: The Desert Dwellers

Ralph Bagnold was a British officer stationed in Egypt between the two world wars. He traveled across the Egyptian deserts using 'light' cars and made many archaeological discoveries. All through his travels, he encountered remains of human settlements in the middle of the empty, hyper-arid desert. The artifacts included many lithic tools, grinding stones, and slabs. In his book *Libyan Sands: Travel in a Dead World*, published in 1935, he muses:

> Who were these people of the Dunes, when they lived, and what it was they ground with their countless grinders, is still a complete mystery. To-day the nearest blade of herbage is hundreds of miles away. The place is utterly devoid of life. Not the least intriguing

aspect of the problem is that they are in use to-day, around the fringes of the desert, grinders which seem identical with the ones found here associated with the tools of Stone Age man. (Bagnold 1935:23)

The mystery, as Bagnold called it, was not to be solved until the 1990s, when direct evidence for ancient vegetation was finally provided through the study of plant remains present in prehistoric sites. Such plant remains are very rare and are preserved only when they are charred and then further protected from erosion by a layer of fine sediments, which are formed in depressions in connection with rainfall. They are also found in and around fire hearths. The recovery, identification, and study of the plant remains in archaeological sites has become a distinct branch of science which is very useful for the study of the mysterious livelihoods and survival strategies of prehistoric communities. This discipline is called paleoethnobotany.

Over the last three decades, paleoethnobotanical research in the Western Desert in Egypt has helped to shed light on aspects of the ancient vegetation and climate of this area in prehistoric times. The research has enabled paleoethnobotanists to reconstruct the environment around the sites and understand subsistence practices for food, shelter, and fuel. There are several well-researched prehistoric sites in the Egyptian Western Desert. The oldest and most extensively studied site is Nabta Playa, 150 kilometers west of Abu Simbel. Nabta is a complex of many sites that were occupied from 6,000 to 9,000 years ago. Other sites include Eastpans, which lies in the Abu Ballas ridge south of Dakhla oasis; radiocarbon analysis dates it to around 6,200 years ago. Another site, called Hidden Valley, lies north of the Farafra oasis and dates to around 6,900 years ago.

The interpretation of the assemblages of plant remains identified from the various sites led to the reconstruction of the environment as a dry savanna, but their use as food presents an interesting perspective discussed in Wasylikowa and Dahlberg (1999:29). This study shows that the food plants from the Nabta site included:

- Wild grasses: *Sorghum bicolor* (wild sorghum), *Echinocloa colona*, *Panicum turgidum*, *Digitaria*, *Setaria*, *Brachiaria*, and *Urochloa*

The Prehistoric Era: The Desert Dwellers

- Seeds, possibly used in similar ways to grasses: *Boerhavia* species and *Scirpus maritimus*
- Fleshy fruits: *Capparis deciduas* (wild caper), *Grewia* species, *Ziziphus* species, *Solanum nigrum* (nightshade), and *Salvadora persica*
- Tubers: *Cyperus rotundus*, *Typha* species, *Nymphaea*, and *Scirpus*
- Leaves: *Astragalus, Boerhavia, Rumex, Schouwia, Solanum nigrum,* and *Salvadora persica*

Comparison of the macroremains from Nabta with those identified from the two other sites (Barakat and Fahmy 1999:40) showed a similar combination of wild grasses in all three sites. They are the most frequent and diverse group, along with other relatively large seeds and rhizomes.

Table 1 shows the presence of wild grasses in the three sites under study.

Table 1. Presence of wild grasses in three prehistoric sites

Plant name	Nabta	Farafra	Abu Ballas
Sorghum species	+	+	+
Panicum turgidum	+	+	+
Echinocloa colona	+	+	+
Setria viridian	+	+	+
Cenchrus/Pennisetum		+	
Brachiaria species		+	+
Digitaria species	+	+	+
Urochloa species	+		+

(Source: Barakat and Fahmy 1999:40)

Ethnographic records for the gathering, harvesting, and consumption of wild grasses in the Sahara and sub-Saharan Africa exist up to the present day in the desert and savanna (Barakat and Fahmy 1999:43). A large number of species are collected and the yield is usually abundant as well as predictable. The most important grasses nowadays are *Panicum* and *Cenchrus*, both found on prehistoric sites. They are highly palatable and can be consumed in a variety of ways.

They are ground to make flour and made into couscous. They are neither famine nor scarcity foods but nourishing staples. Furthermore, the rituals, traditions, and implements used today suggest that they go back to ancient times.

The consistency in results among the sites provides evidence that the inhabitants of the Western Desert 6,000 to 9,000 years ago relied on wild grasses, fruits, rhizomes, legumes, and other herbaceous plants for their food and fodder. It is likely that the plants grew in the vicinity of the sites and were collected and intensively used as food, and that they also grew around lakes formed in the depressions after rainfall, which was estimated to be between 100 and 250 millimeters annually during the wet periods.

Archaeozoological studies of bones has established that the domestication of cattle took place in Egypt around 9,000 years ago (Wendorf et al. 1991:2), while there is no evidence for domestication of plants until much later. The population thus consisted of animal herders gathering wild food plants. From a food perspective, it is highly unlikely that the desert dwellers consumed cattle meat on a regular basis, but they probably used their milk and blood, and the slaughter of animals was linked to rituals as offerings on special occasions.

The onset of arid conditions led to the establishment of the desert about 6,000 years ago. The desert dwellers were forced to move south or east into the Nile Valley, where conditions were by then favorable, and vegetation similar to that found today was available. This marks the beginning of the Predynastic period.

The Predynastic Era: When It All Began

The Predynastic period in Egypt lasted from 6,000 to 5,500 years before the present and witnessed major changes in lifestyle. The inhabitants of the desert had to move to the Nile Valley, where we have the first evidence for agriculture. In fact, the first cultivated grains—wheat and barley—were found on Predynastic sites north of Lake Qaroun in Fayoum. Many other sites along the Nile and in the Delta yielded grains, seeds, and fruits, some cultivated and others wild, all charred and found in settlements or, more rarely, in burials.

Table 2 shows the earliest finds for the various edible plants. Many of the sites contained very diverse archaeobotanical assemblages.

Table 2. Edible plants found at predynastic sites

Latin name	Common name	Status	Predynastic site	Reference
Hordeum sativum	Barley	Cultivated	Fayum	Caton-Thompson and Gardener 1934
Triticum dicoccum	Emmer wheat	Cultivated	Merimde	Werth 1939
Cyperus esculentus	Tigernut	Wild	Badari	Brunton 1927
Pisum sativum	Garden pea	Cultivated	Buto	Thanheiser 1996
Portulaca oleracea	Purslane	Wild/weed	Naqada	Wetterstrom 1984
Trigonella foenum graecum	Fenugreek	Cultivated	Maadi	Zohary and Hopf 1994
Triticum aestivum	Soft wheat	Cultivated	al-Omari	Barakat 1990
Triticum durum	Hard wheat	Cultivated	Adaima	Vartavan 1992
Vicia faba	Broad bean	Cultivated	Merimde	Werth 1939
Vicia ervilia	Bitter vetch	Weed	Buto	Thanheiser 1996
Vicia lutea	Yellow vetch	Weed	Saqqara	Tackholm 1951
Vicia sativa	Common vetch	Cultivated	Maadi	Zohary and Hopf 1994
Cucumis melo	Melon	Cultivated	Maadi	Van Zeist and de Roller 1993
Citrullus lanatus	Watermelon	Cultivated	Saqqara	Germer 1985
Ficus carica	Fig	Cultivated	Maadi	Van Zeist and de Roller 1993
Ficus sycomorus	Sycomore fig	Wild	Badari	Brunton and Caton-Thompson 1928
Vitis vinifera	Grape	Cultivated	Buto	Thanheiser 1996
Ziziphus spinachristi	Christ's thorn	Wild	Adaima	Vartavan 1992

(Source: Vartavan and Asensi Amoros 1997)

The important point here is that wheat and barley do not grow wild in Egypt, nor do beans or peas. Thus, these finds could only mean that the cultivated grains were introduced to Egypt from areas where these plants grow wild and where they were cultivated prior to their arrival in Egypt, the most probable region being the Fertile Crescent. The grains and seeds were then cultivated in Egypt and became staple foods.

Besides the cultivated plants, many edible fruits and vegetables from wild plants were also found among the remains, such as sycamore figs, tigernut rhizomes, and Christ's-thorn fruits. Green leafy plants such as purslane and Jew's mallow were more rarely found in remains, due to their perishable nature.

Although we do not know much about how these food plant assemblages were used, the plants are similar to those known today, and we can assume that the grains of wheat and barley and the seeds of other plants were ground and made into bread. Rhizomes of tigernut could also be used to make bread and cakes. Pulses (beans, peas, and vetches) were cooked, and appreciated for their high protein content. Green leafy plants were added for flavor and to make broth and soups. Fruits were eaten raw, cooked, or dried and stored.

Dynastic Egypt: An Era of Expansion and Diversity

The introduction of many other plants followed during the Dynastic period. Some dynasties were of particular importance in this regard; this was related to expeditions carried out by the kings and queens, the conquering of new lands, trade, and movements of peoples. Table 3 lists plants according to their earliest finds in tombs, mummies, settlements, trash mounds, and kilns. They are classified by dynasty as documented in Vartavan and Asensi Amoros (1997).

From the entire Dynastic era, in addition to the actual plant remains, there is a lot of artistic evidence of plants on walls of tombs and temples. These help complete the picture and sometimes give us insights into how the plants were used, as in the cases of bread-making, wine-making, and beer-brewing.

It is true that utensils have been found among funerary objects, as well as some illustrations for the preparation of meat, baking, wine-making, and brewing. There are even bread samples and residues, and an assemblage that presumably represents a complete funerary meal. Yet we can only assume that the food items found in tombs reflect what was eaten by the deceased, and that funerary tables of offerings depict the real-life way in which plants and animals were consumed. But in fact, except for bread, wine, and beer, there is no documentation, no cookbooks, no recipes. Some experimental archaeobotany has been undertaken by researchers, such as in the cases of bread and beer.

Table 3. Plant remains found during the Dynastic period

Latin name	Common name	Site	Reference	Dynasty
Ceratonia siliqua	Carob	Kahun	Newberry 1890	12
Phoenix dactylifera	Date palm	Dra Abu-l-Naga	Schweinfurth 1885	12
Punica granatum	Pomegranate	Dra Abu-l-Naga	Schweinfurth 1885	12
Allium cepa	Onion	Mummies	Lucas 1962	13
Allium sativum	Garlic	Deir al-Medina	Tackholm 1951	18
Cicer arietinum	Chickpea	Tutankhamun	Vartavan 1990	18
Cucumis sativus	Cucumber	Deir al-Medina	Bruyère 1937	18
Coriandrum sativum	Coriander	Tutankhamun	Lucas 1942	18
Prunus dulcis	Almond	Tutankhamun	Lucas 1942	18
Cuminum sativum	Cumin	Deir al-Medina	Breccia 1927	18
Nigella sativa	Black cumin	Tutankhamun	Newberry 1927	18
Sesamum indicum	Sesame	Deir al-Medina	Germer 1985	18
Apium graveolens	Celery	Deir al-Medina	Newberry 1927	18
Prunus persica	Peach	Hibeh	Wetterstrom 1984	21
Lupinus albus	Lupin	Thebes	Germer 1985	22

(Source: Vartavan and Asensi Amoros 1997)

Bread. It could be very tempting to look for a direct analogy between ancient Egyptian bread and *shamsi* (sun-leavened bread, the precursor of sourdough bread, round or triangular, made of wheat), *bettaw* (flat bread), and similar modern types of bread. However, studies and experimentation with bread-making according to artistic evidence, archaeological material, and examination of ancient bread samples found in museums have revealed a strong resemblance but no exact match. The ancient bread was denser, coarser, and possibly made using malt from sprouted emmer wheat grains. There is also evidence that some flat bread was cooked on the preheated sides of cylindrical ovens (Samuel 2000:569).

Beer. Thorough study and experimentation with beer brewing suggests that there might be direct continuity since ancient times in the case of *bouza* (a fermented drink). Brewing it involves mixing two differently treated batches of grains or lightly baked bread mixed with uncooked malt, but with some alteration in technique between the ancient and the modern processes (Samuel 2000:557).

For most of the other plant remains, we know a lot about what plants were cultivated, and when and how these plants arrived in Egypt, but we know very little about how they were used. We must therefore rely on ethnographic resemblance and socioanthropological similarities with modern Nubian and Egyptian cuisine.

Vegetables. Lettuce, green onions, cucumber, celery, purslane, coriander, cichorium, fenugreek leaves, and green broad beans could have been consumed raw, not necessarily as a 'salad' but on their own or to accompany bread and cheese. Other vegetables, such as the green leaves of cowpea, purslane, carthamus, vetch, cichorium, spinach, mallow, and Jew's mallow, must have been cooked to make green soups and sauces. The tradition of mixing bread with vegetables into the *fatta* of Nubian cuisine (personal communication with Dr. Hoda Yacoub) seems to be a possibility, too, in addition to the combination of pulses and green leafy vegetables.

Pulses. Lentils and sprouted beans (*nabet*) could have been used as a base for making soup (broth) used in cooking other food items, such as vegetables or *fatta*. Broad beans (green or dry) could have been used to make the thick paste of *bessara*.

Grains. Wheat and barley were dominant, alongside some other minor grains. Humans learned how to process grains to make flour, but also other interesting byproducts such as *desheish* (a bulgur-like substance, produced mainly as a result of sieving the milled flour to separate the fine flour for bread). Roasting green wheat and pounding grains produced *fireek* (green roasted crushed wheat), another possible byproduct of wheat processing. These grain products were used instead of rice. A third probable use of grain was to make *kishk* (balls of dry crushed wheat with sour milk).

Fruits. Fruits were consumed raw and also used in cakes. Fig and date cakes are exhibited at The Agricultural Museum in Dokki.

Late Dynasties, Roman, Greek, and Greco-Roman Periods

The late dynasties and the transitional period witnessed a lot of exchange. Some new plants were introduced from the Mediterranean, mostly aromatic herbs and fruits. Some of these plants were cultivated, but others were imported as fruits, such as pine nut, walnut, hazelnut, and possibly pepper during the Roman period, and definitely coconut later on.

Table 4 lists the plant finds known from Greco-Roman and Roman sites.

Table 4. Plants found at Greco-Roman and Roman sites

Latin name	Common name	Site	Reference
Greco-Roman			
Laurus nobilis	Bay leaves	Hawara	Newberry 1889
Origanum majoranum	Sweet marjoram	Douch	Barakat and Baum 1992
Pyrus malus	Apple	Douch	Barakat and Baum 1992
Rosmarinus officinalis	Rosemary	Douch	Barakat and Baum 1992
Roman			
Prunus armeniaca	Apricot	Kellis	Thanheiser 1999
Morus nigra	Mulberry	Hawara	Newberry 1889
Brassica oleracea	Cabbage	Hawara	Newberry 1889
Citrus medica	Lemon	Antinoë	Bonnet 1902

(Source: Vartavan and Asensi Amoros 1997)

During the first century AD an interesting publication was found, perhaps representing the first cookbook. It includes references to several recipes from Alexandria (Apicius 2002:114–115), and mentions the use of black pepper, prunes, vinegar, and olive oil. In fact, Alexandria is usually credited for the lucrative trade with India. After the founding of that city, sailors discovered the monsoons and started to use this wind to reach the Indian subcontinent. During the first century AD, these trips were documented by Pliny, who recorded ships leaving Alexandria for Berenice, thence to Muziris (Mangalore) and back with the south/southwest wind. Imported commodities from India were then carried 258 Roman miles on camels to Coptos, which was connected to the Nile by a canal. The items then went down the Nile to Alexandria.

The Arrival of the Arabs

Although trade in spices with India and the Far East must have started during the Pharaonic era, in the eighteenth century BC, via the Red Sea, the spice routes flourished even more and brought many new food items with the expansion of Islam through Asia and Africa. Egypt seems to have been at the center of almost all the routes as a link between east and west. A surge in the activities of *al-karems* (the spice traders), and in the prices of some of the spices, between the fifth and the eleventh centuries AD has been documented in many publications (al-Ashqar 1991:40). Figure 1 shows the major routes for this trade.

The plants used as spices came from the countries surrounding the Indian Ocean. They included cinnamon, cloves, cardamom, nutmeg, balanos, and peppercorns. The latter became a major item of commerce and were very expensive, as there was no chili pepper in the Old World. From China came ginger and galangan. Egypt was famous for its sugar, but it imported saffron, mastic, salt, olive oil, grains, flour, and fruits from Europe.

Many new plants were introduced and cultivated in Egypt: bananas, rice, sugar cane, asparagus, eggplant, spinach, sumac, lemon, white mulberry, sweet marjoram, jasmine, bitter orange, and sweet orange. Other imported plants never grew successfully in the country, such as coconut, pistachio, hazelnuts, coffee, and tea. During the same period, a surge in animal consumption can be seen, and the chicken was introduced from Persia by the eighth century AD. All this innovation was translated into new food items and activity in the sultan's kitchen through the lavish

The Arrival of the Arabs

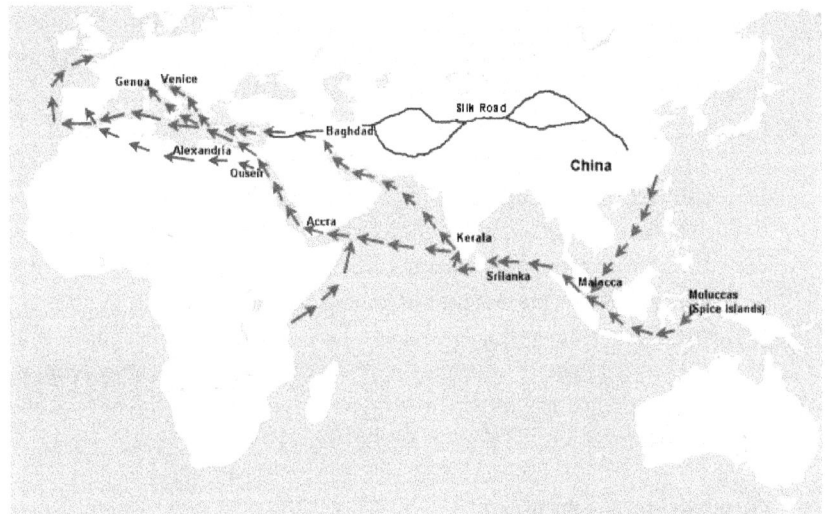

Figure 1. Spice routes (Source: Silk Routes.net, http://www.ipekyollari.net/SilkSpiceIncenseRoutes.htm)

use of spices, meats, and poultry. Meals began to include entrees and sweets, and to be accompanied by etiquette and rituals, all of which is well documented and researched (Abd al-Aziz 1989:7, 11, 12). Even accounts of some of the menus were found. These included:

- *Roz mefalfel*: peppered rice
- *Asfezbag*: meat with chickpeas and spices (kholongan [*Alpinia officinarum*] and cinnamon)
- *Gawazeb*: chicken with saffron and sugar
- *Kamekh*: assorted vegetables with spices as entrees
- Sweets made with rice, milk, and sugar
- *Gawaresh*: mastic sweets, musk sweets
- *Faneed*: cooked concentrated sugar-cane juice
- *Harissa*: a spicy chili-pepper paste with dates and other fruits, pistachio, roses

Further evidence for new plants, foods, and recipes can be found in contemporary cookbooks. The oldest Arabic cookbook, *Kitab al-Tabikh* (The Book of Cooking), dates to the ninth century and was written by

Ibrahim ibn Mahdi (the younger brother of Harun al-Rashid), from Baghdad (Waines 1989:11). *Kitab al-Tabikh* is a formal treatise on food which reflects a large-scale literary movement and a clear interest in the luxuries of life. The manuscript was reworked by D. Waines in his book *In a Caliph's Kitchen*. He also included three recipes from an Egyptian manuscript of unknown date, written in Arabic: the *mu'tamadiya* omelette (whose ingredients include white cheese, black olives, coriander, sumac, cinnamon, pepper, lamb, chicken, and eggs), eggplant patties or omelette (whose ingredients include green peppercorns, cinnamon, red wine vinegar, olive oil, sumac, coriander, bread crumbs, garlic, and eggplant), and sumac fish (using the fruits of *Rhus tripartita* growing in the mountainous areas around the Mediterranean, plus *tahini* [sesame paste] and lemon juice) (Waines 1989:100, 110).

Discovering the Americas

In the history of the spice trade, the *karems* referred to earlier were in charge of the entire trade in spices, luxury goods, and many other food items during the Fatimid era. They flourished under the Ayyubids, continued during the Crusades, and were protected by the Mamluk sultans at the beginning of their reign. However, the Mamluks later imposed taxes on the spice traders and eventually took over the business. By the beginning of the sixteenth century AD, Portuguese traders had begun to compete with the *karems*. Coupled with the Mamluks' antagonism, this eventually led to the collapse of the *karems*' trade in the Orient.

The rise of Portugal as a naval power encouraged Portuguese sailors to find new routes to reach India, thus avoiding the old spice routes and securing the trade in spices and other goods for themselves. The most famous of these voyages are those of Christopher Columbus, which might seem like a failed expedition, as he accidentally stumbled on the 'New World' while looking for the Far East. To compensate for his failure, he brought back to Europe many of the plants he found in his presumed 'fabled Orient,' introducing to the Old World an amazing array of fruits, nuts, grains, and tubers. Many of these plants spread quickly after they arrived in the Mediterranean countries, were cultivated in Europe, and became integrated into the cuisine. Others took much longer to settle down; some of these eventually became staple foods (Foster and Cordell 1992:163).

Much more work needs to be done before we can trace when, how, and why American plants arrived in Egypt and how they have been integrated into the cuisine. The following list contains the plants we know, use, and cultivate or still import, arranged chronologically according to my observations of how Egyptian cuisine evolved.

First wave: *Phaseolus vulgaris* (common beans), *Capsicum* species (chili pepper), *Cucurbita pepo* (pumpkin), *Cucurbita pepo* var. *pepo* (zucchini), *Solanum lycopersum* (tomato), *Helianthus annuus* (sunflower), *Ipomoea batatas* (sweet potato), *Zea mays* (maize), *Arachis hypogaea* (peanut), *Solanum tuberosum* (potato), *Psidium guajava* (guava), *Opuntia* species (prickly pear).

Late arrivals: *Physalis peruviana* (cape gooseberry, golden berry), *Annona cherimola* (cherimoya), *Carica papaya* (papaya), *Diospyrus virginiana* (persimmon), *Persea americana* (avocado), *Passiflora* species (passion fruit), *Carya illinoinensis* (pecan), *Lippia* species (Mexican oregano), *Fragaria x ananassa:* (strawberry hybrid), *Simmondsia chinensis* (jojoba), *Chenopodium quinoa* (quinoa).

Imported plants: *Bertholettia excelsa* (Brazil nut), *Theobroma cacao* (cacao), *Anacardium occidentale* (cashew), *Ananas comosus* (pineapple), *Vanilla planifolia* (vanilla).

The Ottomans, the French, and the British: The Legacy of the Modern Egyptian Cuisine

It is fascinating to see how this cuisine was a rich melting pot of Egyptian, Turkish, and European cuisines. Niqola and Othman were aware of these influences, and sometimes referred to a dish or an ingredient in a recipe as foreign (*afrangi*) or by its specific country of origin (French, Italian, English, or Russian). They wrote their book for the younger generation of women, to help educate the future mothers in Egypt in the theory and practice of modern cooking. The book is a collection of traditional as well as new and foreign dishes. For example, in the chapters on baked goods, there are recipes for many different types of bread, from *baladi* (regular whole-wheat bread) to sourdough to baguette. In the cakes chapter, *fateer al-rahma* (ritual

The cookbook entitled *Osul al-tahi al-nazari wa-l-'amali* (The Basics of Theoretical and Practical Cooking) is perhaps the best representation of the evolution of Egyptian cuisine as influenced by the Ottoman, French, and British occupations of Egypt. Nazeera Niqola first published her 900-page textbook in 1942 in collaboration with Baheya Othman. The 13th edition, published in 1981, is the one I used in my research. It contains almost 1,800 recipes, covering all the known cooked foods in Egypt at that time.

cakes) are seamlessly followed by whole-wheat scones or Christmas cake. Also, very much ahead of their time, a chapter is dedicated to vegetarian food.

This cuisine is still the Egyptian food that people cook and consume in their homes, in spite of all the changes that have occurred during the last 50 years. These changes would be a good subject for further research.

Conclusions

The globalization of our food system started some 6,000 years ago, and most of the foods we eat today, both plant and animal, have been introduced from all over the world. This global phenomenon is particularly clear in the Egyptian context. As these plants and animals were cultivated and domesticated in the country, they have shaped our food practices and eventually became our 'food heritage.' This fact should encourage us to reconsider the notion of 'local' and 'national' versus 'foreign' and 'international' foods, ingredients, and cuisines, and even the very notion of a country's 'food heritage.' In the case of Egypt, much more research is needed to trace, document, and understand how the cuisine has evolved, especially during the last 500 years, to bring us to what we consider today as our 'Egyptian' cuisine.

References

Abd al-Aziz, N. M. 1989. *al-Matbakh al-sultani zaman al-Ayubiyin wa-l-Mamlik*. Cairo: Anglo-Egyptian Bookshop.

Apicius. 2002. *Art Culinaire*. Trans. J. André. Paris: Les belles lettres.

al-Ashqar, M. A. 1991. *Togar al-tawabel fi Misr fi al-'asr al-mamluki*. Cairo: Egyptian General Book Organization.

Bagnold, R. A. 1935. *Libyan Sands: Travel in a Dead World*. Reprint 1978. London: Michael Haag.

Barakat, H. 1990. "Plant Remains from El Omari." In F. Debono and B. Mortensen, eds., *El Omari: A Neolithic Settlement and Other Sites in the Vicinity of Wadi Hof, Helwan*, 109–116. Archäologische Veröffentlichungen (Deutsches Archäologisches Institut, Abteilung Kairo) 82. Mainz: Philipp von Zabern.

Barakat, H. N., and N. Baum. 1992. *La végétation antique de Douch: Une approche macrobotanique (Douch II)*. Cairo: Institut Français d'Archéologie Orientale.

Barakat, H., and G. el-Din Fahmy. 1999. "Wild Grasses as 'Neolithic' Food Resources in the Eastern Sahara." In M. van der Veen, ed., *The Exploitation of Plant Resources in Ancient Africa*. 33–46. New York: Kluwer Academic/Plenum Publishers.

Bonnet, E. 1902. "Plantes antiques des nécropoles d'Antinoë," *Journal de Botanique*, 16(9): 1–6.

Breccia, E. 1927. "La Missione Archeologica Italiana in Egitto e la tombe intata dell'Architetto Cha," *Emporium*, 66(393): 1–8.
Brunton, G. 1927. *Qau and Badari I*. British School of Archaeology in Egypt & Egyptian Research Account 44. London.
Brunton, G., and G. Caton-Thompson. 1928. *The Badarian Civilization and Predynastic Remains near Badari*. London: Bernard Quarich.
Bruyère, B. 1937. *Rapport sur les fouilles de Deir El Medineh (1934–1935). Deuxième partie: la nécropole de l'Est*. Fouilles de l'Institut Français du Caire 15. Cairo: Institut Français d'Archéologie Orientale.
Caton-Thompson, G., and E. W. Gardener. 1934. *The Desert Fayum*. London: Royal Anthropological Institute of Great Britain and Ireland.
Foster, N., and L. S. Cordell, eds. 1992. *Chilies to Chocolate*. Tucson: University of Arizona Press.
Germer, R. 1985. *Flora des Pharaonischen Ägypten*. Mainz: Philipp von Zabern.
Lucas, A. 1942. "Notes on Some of the Objects from the Tomb of Tutankhamun," *Annales du Service des Antiquités Egyptiennes*, 41: 135–147.
———. 1962. *Ancient Egyptian Materials and Industries*. London: Arnold.
Newberry, P. E. 1889. "On the Vegetable Remains Discovered in the Cemetery of Hawara." In W. M. F. Petrie, ed., *Hawara, Biahnu and Arsinoe*, 46–53. London: Field & Tuer, The Leadenhall Press.
———. 1890. "The Ancient Botany." In W. F. Petrie, ed., *Kahun, Gurob and Hawara*, 46–50. London: Kegan Paul, Trench, Trubner and Co.
———. 1927. "Report on the Floral Wreaths Found in the Coffins of Tut-Ankh-Amen." In H. Carter, ed., *The Tomb of Tutankhamen*, 2:39, 2:189–196. London: Cassel and Company.
Niqola, N., and B. Othman. 1942. *Osul al-tahi al-nazari wa-l-'amali*. 13th rev. ed. Cairo: Maktabet al-Nahda al-Misriya.
Samuel, D. 2000. "Brewing and Baking." In P. T. Nicholson and I. Shaw, eds., *Ancient Egyptian Materials and Technology*, 537–576. Cambridge, UK: Cambridge University Press.
Schweinfurth, G. 1885. "Notice sur les restes de végétaux de l'ancienne Egypte: Contenus dans une armoire du Musée de Boulaq," *Bulletin de l'Institut Egyptien* series 2, 5: 3–10.

Tackholm, V. 1951. *Faraos blomster*. Stockholm: Natur och Kultur.
Thanheiser, U. 1996. "Local Production versus Import of Cereals during the Predynastic Period in the Nile Delta (Tell Ibrahim Awad and Tell el Fara'in/Buto)." In K. Krzyzaniak, K. Kroeper, and M. Kobusiewicz, eds., *Interregional Contacts in the Later Prehistory of Northeastern Africa*. Poznan: Poznan Archaeological Museum.
———. 1999. "Plant Remains from Kellis, First Results." In C. A. Hope and A. J. Mills, eds., *Dakhleh Oasis Project: Preliminary Reports on the 1992–1993 and 1993–1994 Field Seasons*. Oxford: Oxbow Books.
Vartavan, C. de. 1990. "Contaminated Plant-foods from the Tomb of Tutankhamun: A New Interpretive System," *Journal of Archaeological Science*, 17: 473–494.
———. 1992. "Rapport préliminaire sur les restes végétaux d'Adaïma," *Bulletin de l'Institut Français d'Archéologie Orientale*, 91: 243–246.
Vartavan, C. de, and V. Asensi Amoros. 1997. *Codex of Ancient Egyptian Plant Remains*. London: Triade Exploration.
Waines, D. 1989. *In a Caliph's Kitchen*. London: Riad El Rayyes Books.
Wasylikowa, K., and J. Dahlberg. 1999. "Sorghum in the Economy of the Early Neolithic Nomadic Tribes at Nabta Playa, Southern Egypt." In M. van der Veen, ed., *The Exploitation of Plant Resources in Ancient Africa*, 11–31. London: Kluwer Academic/Plenum Publishers.
Wendorf, F., A. E. Close, R. Schild, and K. Wasylikowa. 1991. "The Combined Prehistoric Expedition Results of the 1990 and 1991 Seasons," *Newsletter of the American Research Center in Egypt*, 154: 1–8.
Werth, E. 1939. "Emmer und Gerste aus dem 5. Jahrtausend v. Chr. und andere vorgeschichtliche Kulturpflanzen," *Bericht der deutschen botanischen Gesellschaft*, 57(9): 453–462.
Wetterstrom, W. 1984. "The Plant Remains." In R. S. Wenke, ed., *Archaeological Investigations at El-Hibeh: Preliminary Report*, 50–75. ARCE Reports 9. Malibu: Undena Publications.
Zeist, W. van, and G. J. de Roller. 1993. "Plant Remains from Maadi: A Predynastic Site in Lower Egypt," *Vegetation History and Archaeobotany*, 2: 1–14.
Zohary, D., and M. Hopf. 1994. *Domestication of Plants in the Old World*. Oxford: Clarendon Press.

CHAPTER 3

Killing Them Softly: Dietary Deficiencies and Food Insecurity in Twentieth-Century Egypt

Ellis Goldberg

Introduction

The spread and decline of pellagra, a debilitating and sometimes deadly disease, in Egypt between 1840 and 1960 provides a unique view of the intersection of technology transfer, government fiscal policy, unequal income distribution, and increased mortality and morbidity.[1] Telling this story shows that disease can be assimilated to the causal mechanisms elucidated by Amartya Sen in his study of hunger and death during the great famines of the nineteenth and twentieth centuries. This story also illuminates the danger of relying on nostalgic visions of the past as an era of 'food security.' It is furthermore a story about the need to recognize that foodstuffs—including grain—are not simple items in the natural world. Rather, like other commodities, they are envelopes of a technology whose transfer requires far more complex adaptation than physical exchange. This part of the story is especially intriguing because the technology of maize in the Old World utilized only a portion of its preparation as a nutrient already available in the New World at the time of the European conquests known as the 'Columbian Exchange.'

As with many diseases, there are numerous technological solutions to pellagra, but the social processes through which one is chosen are far from simple. Republican Egypt opted for one solution: subsidized provision of an imported higher-status food to replace maize. There were others. Wheat subsidies and imports have attracted much criticism

---

1 Pellagra manifests through skin lesions and rashes as well as loss of appetite and weight. It can also include diarrhea, irritability, delirium, and dementia.

since at least the 1980s for reasons as diverse as their impact on the state budget, national balance of payments, dietary deficiency, corruption, and food security. The history behind and before them tells us that the proposed cures for these asserted ills may be worse than the fiscal or cultural ills they diagnose.

This chapter is organized into four parts. First, I discuss pellagra as a disease in Egypt and elsewhere, as well as the emerging expert consensus about its cause and cure. I then address the issue of why consumption of maize was not related to pellagra in pre-Columbian America and the utility of seeing maize as one element in a food technology rather than simply as a single natural substance. Third, I discuss the spread of maize in nineteenth- and twentieth-century Egypt as a food that enhanced the self-sufficiency of rural inhabitants in a period when neither the state nor the market provided support for increasing their dietary well-being. Fourth, I discuss the decision of the post-1952 regime to provide Egyptians with a grain of perceived higher nutritional value and prestige and the long-term effects of this decision on public health and the public budget. I conclude with an examination of some of the debates about Egyptian food policy and the likely impacts of attempting to achieve food security if that means both national and individual self-sufficiency in food production. Attempts by analysts as diverse as Timothy Mitchell and Alan Richards to think about Egypt and food have real shortcomings, both because they fail to understand grain in terms of food technology and because they fail, in different ways, to appreciate how food markets work.

Between 1880 and 1950, although Egypt was largely self-sufficient in food, wheat was not the dominant cereal in rural Egypt. Egyptian self-sufficiency, by which we mean low imports, in food relied to a large degree on corn (maize) production. Corn consumption was connected to large and important negative impacts on health in Egypt as well as Italy, southeastern Europe, and many parts of the American South. Along with other changes, the shift to wheat, which was increasingly imported, in the mid twentieth century played a role in alleviating these impacts.

Because these negative health impacts had not been apparent in the New World, where corn originated, the shift between cereals in Egypt also suggests some issues with modern technology transfer. For comparative purposes I therefore briefly discuss the transfer of another agricultural technology from the New World to the Old—the potato and its impact on Ireland. These two examples help us understand the ways in which markets for goods and labor can interact and negatively affect technology transfer. They also suggest that the search for self-sufficiency is not likely to resolve the issues of food provision and diet even if it were to resolve problems of state finance. Export-oriented agricultural policies that result in larger incomes for poorer farmers may be a more plausible way to resolve both the macroeconomic and health risks a country like Egypt faces, but will not necessarily do so.

Wheat is native to the Middle East and has been grown in Egypt since ancient times. For the first half of the nineteenth century Egypt was, on balance, a wheat exporter, but this changed in the wake of the cotton boom during the American Civil War. Just before the First World War, Egypt had come to rely on imported wheat for a significant portion of its bread, but the reliance on imports of flour and wheat was not seen as a significant problem financially or strategically before the Second World War.

Despite the very long history of wheat production and consumption in the Nile Valley and despite its present dominance, by the late nineteenth and early twentieth centuries wheat was no longer the dominant food for Egyptians. Maize, a cereal developed in the Tehuacán Valley of Mexico, had become the primary food for rural Egyptians by the middle of the nineteenth century and possibly earlier.[2] Maize employs oxygen and water more efficiently than wheat and requires less labor. It is therefore less expensive to produce, and it spread rapidly across the Old World after its introduction from the Americas in the early sixteenth century.

Maize allowed Egyptian peasants to be self-sufficient in food production. As agricultural specialization and global trade in agricultural products grew in the nineteenth century, maize allowed the production of export-oriented agriculture without the requirement for compensating imports of food. Thus, Egypt was self-sufficient in food while at the

---

2 "Corn and dourah, a kind of sorghum, are two plants which play a special role in the agriculture of Egypt, in the sense that they are those which furnish for the peasant the greater part of his food" (Barois 1889:84). See also Alan Richards, discussing Egypt between 1880 and 1914: "Peasants had to assure themselves an adequate supply of two principal foodstuffs, maize and beans" (1982:83).

same time exporting increasingly specialized agricultural goods, mainly extra-long staple cotton. Whatever financial problems Egypt had before the Second World War, they were not primarily related to current consumption. On the contrary, they were connected to investment and frequently to infrastructural investment such as the Suez Canal, rail transport, or urban improvements.

Egyptian self-sufficiency in food may have conferred financial benefits on the state, but because of how self-sufficiency was achieved it was closely connected to severe health problems. From at least the middle of the nineteenth to the middle of the twentieth century, rural Egyptians grew the corn that provided the bulk of their diet. In the last two centuries, at least outside Central America, corn consumption has been linked to the spread of pellagra, a debilitating and life-threatening disease. Pellagra manifests in an enlarged and weakened heart, diarrhea, mental confusion, edema, ataxia, and dementia. Untreated, it can lead to death within four to five years of onset. Although it was long known that pellagra was related to the consumption of maize, the exact mechanisms causing pellagra were not discovered until around the Second World War. For about forty years it was epidemic in much of the American South and the Mediterranean basin as well as many parts of Asia and Africa.

Pellagra

Pellagra is now usually understood to be the result of niacin (frequently known as nicotinic acid) deficiency, although there is evidence for a different causal chain (FAO 1992, "Lime-treated Maize"). The association of maize and pellagra was recognized almost as soon as the disease was first identified, in 1735 in Italy, but the causal mechanism involved was unknown (Mariani-Costantini and Mariani-Costantini 2007:165). The earliest published description of pellagra in Egypt in 1846 described the symptoms, noted that it was not infectious, and linked its appearance to consumption of maize as well as lack of sanitation, starvation, and impure water.[3] Describing pellagra as a disease in an era when the germ theory of disease was at the cutting edge of

---

3 "The Earliest Account of Pellagra from the Writings of an Egyptian Physician, A.D. 1846," April 3, 1922. *Proceedings of the Royal Society of Medicine (Tropical Disease and Parasitology Section*, 45-47, partial translation of A. H. El-Rashidy, "Diseases of the Skin" (Cairo: Boulaq, 1846) [Arabic].

medical science implied that a specific agent caused it. Research centered on the search for such an agent.[4]

The puzzle, as it was then understood, was that although consumption of maize and pellagra were related, there were people who exhibited pellagra who ate no maize and people who ate maize as their principal cereal and never contracted pellagra. Clearly, American Indians had eaten maize for thousands of years without suffering from pellagra, whereas significant numbers of Europeans, Africans, and Asians had begun to suffer from pellagra within a hundred years of its introduction.

There were advocates for what we might now call a 'social constructionist' view of pellagra who argued that it was a disease of the poor and poorly nourished for whom some as yet unidentified nutritional elements were lacking (Perdue in Alessandrini and Scala 1916:315). Researchers continued to be puzzled by it for years. As one scholarly monograph put it in 1916, "the most prominent theory of the cause of pellagra is the eating of corn meal" (Alessandrini and Scala, Part 1, 1916:313). The hypothesis that maize itself or spoiled maize caused pellagra arose nearly with the onset of the disease itself. Alessandrini and Scala, as well as Perdue, conducted clinical trials on animals and also gathered impressionistic correlational material to establish what they believed was a more scientific causal connection: "Pellagra is a chronic acid intoxication caused by colloidal silica in the water supply. Pellagra is strictly localized and contracted in those areas where the water supply is derived from clay soils" (Perdue in Alessandrini and Scala, Part 2, 1916:318). In a presidential address to the Society of Tropical Medicine and Hygiene, F. M. Sandwith argued that his own experience at Qasr al-Aini hospital in Cairo, and associated research, indicated that pellagra was a disease of dietary deficiency, notably "vitamines." Sandwith compared pellagra to scurvy and beriberi, which were already understood to be related to diet. Crucial to Sandwith's argument was the observation that "pellagra in Egypt was confined to the poorest Egyptians, most agricultural laborers, with a decided sprinkling of lunatics" (Sandwith

---

4 See Roberts (1914) for a lengthy discussion of theories despite his recognition that the cause was then unknown ("Cause of Pellagra," 231–265). Roberts includes then widely discussed "corn theories" and "water theories" as well as several infectious-agent and ecological theories. Because the major dispute centered on whether pellagra was a maize-caused disease, Rogers described competing theories as either Zeist or anti-Zeist, derived from the scientific name of corn: *Zea mays*.

1915:4). It had already been understood that pellagra was a rural problem, for as one prominent synthetic study argued, it stopped at the gates of cities and urban institutions such as hospitals, asylums, and prisons.

The incidence of pellagra in the Egyptian population as a whole in the late nineteenth century is unknown. In 1914 the subdirector of the Abbasiya Hospital for the Insane noted that between 1896 and 1911, 993 patients had been admitted to the hospital alone for "pellagrous insanity."[5] The same report suggests that (unfortunately unquantified) "numbers of children of the ages 10 to 15 years, dwarfed, cachectic, anemic and having distinct black pellagric rashes" had been observed by another physician. In 1952, a study indicated that between 9 percent and 12 percent of children (5–9 years old) and 12 percent to 21 percent of youth (10–19 years old) in Qalyub suffered from pellagra. For the population as a whole, pellagra was thought to affect between 1 and 7 percent of the inhabitants of the Delta villages.

There is no reason to think that rates had been lower for the earlier half century. Pellagra may have remained common into the 1960s, but by the 1970s it had ceased to be a widespread public health issue. Alan Richards indirectly cites a Cairo University Medical School study from the 1930s suggesting that pellagra affected one-third of the population of the Delta at that time (Richards 1982:161).

Pellagra was already widespread in Egypt but, during the First World War, the country became the site of an unlikely 'natural experiment.' There were thousands of German and Turkish prisoners of war in Egypt. The American medical journal, *The Journal of the American Medical Association*, published an account derived from the British journal, *The Lancet*, of the thousands of cases of pellagra among the prisoners, accompanied by hundreds of necropsies. Turks, rather than Germans, suffered from pellagra, and the one clear difference in the treatment of the two groups was that the Germans had money to buy additional food. The Turkish prisoners ate mainly maize, barley, and wheat ("Pellagra in Egypt," 1920:321). The role of diet, and especially of a diet largely centered on maize, was becoming clear and was reinforced by Joseph Goldberger's research.

In addition to the problem of bioavailability of niacin, the protein in maize is low in lysine and tryptophan (FAO 1992, "Gross Chemical

---

5 Pearson 1914:203. Pellagrous insanity probably refers to dementia, a severe long-term consequence of pellagra.

Composition"). Maize consumption can be linked to the prevalence of kwashiorkor, a protein deficiency. Although wheat does not contain, on average, more protein than maize, that protein is more complete, and therefore wheat can be thought of as a superior food to maize (Young and Pellett 1985). Regardless of nutrition, in places where wheat has long been part of the diet and where it continued to be eaten by those who could afford to, it was considered a higher-status grain.

Maize in the New World

Maize was the dominant New World grain, the most widely cultivated grain or pseudo-grain.[6] Domestication appears to have occurred around 7,000 years ago, roughly contemporaneously with wheat in the Old World. Native Americans do not seem to have deliberately developed maize from teosinte, but they ultimately cultivated a genetically diverse set of plants for many different purposes, from edible corn on the cob, through so-called 'flint' corns, to hard popcorns.

Mesoamericans developed many uses for edible maize. Although maize (like rice) lacks gluten, Native Americans made it into a kind of bread (tortilla) that resembles the flat breads of the Middle East. It also served as the basis for a food that resembles a dumpling (tamale). It can be used for stew (*pozole*) and a beer-like alcoholic beverage (*chicha*). Maize, like wheat, served as the basis for many different foods in a variety of cuisines. We generally think of it as a simple natural object (a grain) that is processed in a variety of different ways.

Before being ground into flour, maize in the New World was almost invariably subjected to 'nixtamalization.' The process appears to be almost as old as domesticated maize and is derived from the Nahuatl words meaning 'ashes' and 'corn dough.' In nixtamalization maize kernels are soaked in lime (an alkali solution) to remove the outer shell or pericarp.[7] Europeans who adopted maize did not adopt nixtamalization and consequently it plays no role in Old World maize cuisine.[8] In maize untreated

---

6 There were other grains and pseudo-grains, notably wild rice and quinoa, but these foods were never widely adopted beyond their initial distributions.

7 There is one indigenous American maize preparation from Venezuela, the *arepa*, that does not include nixtamalization. For *arepa* flour the grain is soaked, peeled, and ground, but not treated with lime. Thus the pericarp is removed but the grain itself is not chemically affected.

8 The one exception is the preparation of hominy and hominy grits in the American South.

by nixtamalization, the niacin is insufficiently bioavailable to meet human needs. Populations that rely heavily on corn but do not engage in nixtamalization are at severe risk for pellagra. Nixtamalized maize tortillas have more calcium than untreated maize as well as somewhat better protein amino acid availability (FAO 1992, "Lime-treated Maize").

Although maize was adopted nearly universally by New World societies, it was adopted unevenly. In midwestern and southeastern North America, maize was only widely adopted in late pre-Columbian times. As elsewhere, human beings did not uniformly make the transition to a cultivated cereal-based diet. Maize had nutritional and other dietary disadvantages compared to pre-existing horticultural diets and also required additional labor and fertilizer (Reber 2006:237).

As one example, we know that maize was the primary food source for the Mesoamerican Mayan societies. Where it appears inland it accounted for perhaps 75 percent of the diet, and somewhat less near the coast. As recent studies have shown, "high levels of maize consumption do not appear to have compromised the health of the Maya," at least in part because they had access to fish, marine foods, and game as well as nixtamalization (Schwarcz 2006:319).

Maize in Egypt

The prominent economic historian Roger Owen argued that maize cultivation spread in Egypt in the eighteenth century, and Kenneth Cuno cites Jabarti to the effect that it was already the peasant staple by the early nineteenth century.[9] It was clearly the dominant food in the countryside after the cotton boom and until the mid twentieth century. Richards argues that maize production increased with perennial irrigation and that it was grown along with cotton. Maize acreage fluctuated in the first decade of the twentieth century but the overall trend in absolute and relative numbers was upward. During these decades maize became the dominant food for peasants (especially in the Delta), who formed the majority of the country's population.

Surprisingly, although maize and cotton were planted in the same season, increased demand for cotton as an export good did not diminish the area of maize. Wheat production did, however, decrease during this

---

9 Cuno (1992:122), where peasant resistance to the timing of corvée labor is connected to the maize-growing season; see also pp. 60, 28, 144.

period. At least one reason lies in the relative cheapness of maize: one unit of cotton could buy more maize than wheat. In addition, because maize required less labor than wheat it was an attractive crop for farmers, who were expected to produce their own food on cotton estates and whose money income from cotton was subject to significant oversight by owners. In other words, family labor was constrained by estate owners and economizing on the production of cheap food was a common response.

Clearly, maize was the dominant food grain in the Egyptian countryside by the late nineteenth century and remained so for the first half of the twentieth century. Before the Second World War, Egypt produced more maize than wheat, both because somewhat more land was planted in maize and because maize produced more grain per unit of land than did wheat.[10] Alan Richards argues that increasing maize yields in the early twentieth century made it an increasingly important part of rural production as well as diet.[11] Increasing yields mattered but only in the context of Egyptian government agricultural policy.

Egypt was self-sufficient in cereals in the 1930s. This was not because agricultural countries are naturally self-sufficient, but because in 1930 the government imposed a prohibitively high tariff on imports and began to subsidize loans for wheat production as well as exports (Issawi 1947:69). Maize imports, for example, were held at around 1 percent of the variation between high and low production; they were not allowed to make up for shortfalls, in other words. The overall effects, as Charles Issawi noted, were perverse and dangerous:

As the bulk of the wheat crop is consumed by the urban proletariat, whose expenditure on bread represents over 50 percent of their budget . . . the town workers have been paying a subsidy of some £E 5,000,000 per annum to the landlords and their tenants. . . . [moreover] the quantity of wheat available for consumption in 1934 was reduced by 40 percent by the tariff and that of maize over 25 per cent in 1933. In a country

---

10 Issawi (1947:63, 68). See also Ayrout (2005:60–61), who proposes "representative" consumption lists indicating the dominance of maize in peasant diets.
11 Richards (1982:83–84). It is possible that the shift, by poorer farmers, to a two-year rotation that Richards discusses was driven by the decision to produce more carbohydrates through maize, even at the expense of beans (production of which decreased) or through the production of marketed commodities to exchange for food.

where the mass of the population is living on the verge of starvation such decreases cannot possibly be justified. (Issawi 1947:69)

Rationing was introduced during the Second World War and grain imports were once again allowed. Between the end of the war and 1955 the commercial market handled wheat imports. Thus, "in 1951, imported wheat constituted nearly 50 percent of the available supply, whereas in 1954 and 1955 the country had a small exportable surplus" (Blue et al. 1983:7). The surplus was the result, so frequently observed in Egyptian agriculture, of farmers responding very quickly to financial incentives (Goldberg 2006:189).[12] In 1952 the government had increased prices and elicited increased yields and areas under cultivation of wheat (Blue et al. 1983:7; see also Goldberg 2006). The availability of cheap American wheat under the P.L. 480 law allowed the Egyptian government to import significant quantities of wheat between 1957 and 1966 and then again after 1975.

We can draw a few inferences from that decade's experience. At least before the 1960s, wheat was a more expensive and more desirable food, consumed primarily in the cities. Maize, on the other hand, was a cheaper and less desirable food. Even if peasants grew wheat they could not necessarily afford to eat it. Consequently, in a regime of forced national self-sufficiency there is no reason necessarily to believe that all Egyptians will have equal access to food. To the contrary, without extensive government regulation it is quite possible that food would be unequally shared in Egypt in terms of both quantity and quality.

Egyptians consumed wheat and maize mainly as ingredients in prepared foods. Wheat was primarily eaten in the form of bread but more recently it has included pasta. Maize was the primary ingredient in rural breads well into the 1960s. Thus one 1956 report says, "the staple food in the Delta is a maize bread which has the appearance of a thin pancake about 14 in. in diameter. White-maize flour (about 96% extraction) to which about 3% of fenugreek is added."[13] The report argues that rural

---

12 As Goldberg (2006) shows with regard to the shift away from Ashmuni cotton to Sakellaridis and then away from Sakellaridis between 1910 and 1920, Egyptian farmers responded to price signals with alacrity.

13 See, for example, Ross (1956:31). Although Ross does not use the term, this appears to be *aish mehrahrah*, which resembles Venezuelan *arepas* rather than tortillas.

families did not eat fava beans (which provide supplementary proteins maize lacks) to the same degree as urban families because they lacked sufficient fuel to cook the beans (Ross 1956:32).

When the military seized power in 1952, the majority of the Egyptian population lived in the countryside and many of them suffered from pellagra. This was due to diets overwhelmingly dominated by maize. It is a whimsical counterfactual consideration to imagine that the Free Officers could have transformed rural Egypt's dietary deficiencies by propagating nixtamalization and encouraging peasants to eat tortillas rather than 'pita' bread. In light of the wholesale adoption by Syro-Lebanese re-emigrants of the rituals of drinking *mate* from the leaves to the gourd and even the little silver straw, it might seem plausible that the entire technology of maize preparation, including *metates*, could have been imported from the New World by a revolutionary government (Folch 2010, especially pp. 6 and 29). Whether a government committed to emulating the advanced capitalist economies could have been convinced to adopt an essentially Neolithic technique is one question. Another is whether Nasser's or any other government would have paid such attention to a technology that it would have been quick to dismiss as women's work. It was never considered and we will never know. The closest anyone in Egypt comes to eating tortillas today are in bags of chips or small boxes of highly commercialized products sold to exceptionally well-off customers who want to eat exotic food—effectively slightly different preparations of the beans, spices, and white cheese that are already common in the diet of many Egyptians.

The choice to convert the diet of many rural Egyptians to wheat was a more obvious one. Not only is niacin more available in wheat than in maize, but wheat also has more available protein than maize. In 1950, two years before the coup, the government decided to import wheat. Because the country had acquired significant reserves of sterling it could afford to import half a million tons.

Imports grew during the Nasser period, but they were not seen as a foreign-exchange problem for a country whose major balance-of-payments issue was spending unconvertible sterling. There are no accounts of why Egyptian governments chose to provide the rural population with a higher quality cereal and, over the next two decades, to transform the

Egyptian diet in the countryside. Government archives may contain information about policy choices and debates, but there is no doubt expert discussions were well under way. In 1954 the new military government requested the World Health Organization to send a study team, which recommended adding nicotinic acid to maize (Patwardhan and Darby 1972:289). Even before the coup, however, Egyptian governments were actively engaged in directly feeding the population as well as regulating food supply. In 1942 the Wafd government legislated free feeding at elementary schools that reportedly provided 125,000 children with bread, cheese, and beans (Patwardhan and Darby 1972:293). By 1951 the Egyptian government may have been feeding two million children at schools, but under the new regime the program was gradually abandoned. Before it ended in 1960 the program had shrunk to the provision of bread alone from US surplus wheat exports (Patwardhan and Darby 1972:294). Adult industrial workers fared better because after 1961 factories employing more than 25 were required to provide highly subsidized meals in canteens (Patwardhan and Darby 1972:298–299).

Although he cites no evidence, Galal describes "major consumer education efforts to decrease the dependence on corn" in the 1950s. He is correct to assert that "pellagra has disappeared in Egypt as a result of the shift towards wheat consumption and general improvement in the availability of animal products" (Galal 2002:143).

International trade in grain in the 1950s and 1960s was centered on wheat for human consumption. This was especially so for three reasons: the US had significant wheat surplus to its domestic demand, demand for maize was primarily as an animal feed, and consequently most maize grown for export was not intended for human consumption (Commonwealth Economic Committee 1965:14). During the 1940s the US government had chosen to pursue the enrichment of white flour as a way of ensuring civilian populations received nutrients that processing had removed. By 1954 a World Health Organization report had recommended fortification of maize flour in Egypt, but this was not carried out (Patwardhan and Darby 1972:289). The importation of wheat, coupled with what Osman describes as "major consumer education efforts to decrease the dependence on corn," was the government's preferred strategy (Galal 2002:143).

The decision to subsidize wheat (and other food products) had several motivations. "Subsidies," as the late Iliya Harik wrote, "may well have started in Egypt as a support system for the urban poor, but in a patron state such as Egypt they amounted to a monetary policy whose objective was to adjust wages and prices" (Harik 1992:481). Nevertheless, food subsidies, as Bent Hansen argued at around the same time, "have been a major tool of income distribution policy since 1973" (Hansen 1991:226). Subsidies, as Harik noted, provide compensation in kind and therefore reduce the pressure on employers (including the state) to adjust wages upward and employment downward. Thus, the subsidy system allowed the state (then a major employer) to provide a large number of jobs at very low wages (Alderman, von Braun, and Sakr 1982:15). As was well known early in the Mubarak era, food subsidies were nearly equitable: the poorest 27 percent of the population received 22 percent of the food subsidy; the wealthiest 21 percent received 27 percent of the subsidy, mainly through their purchases of high-cost products such as meat and edible oils. Far more important and also far more unequal were the energy subsidies, which even by 1990 were dramatically skewed to better-off Egyptians: the top 21 percent of the population received 70 percent of the energy subsidy (Harik 1992:489).

Subsidized food (and other goods) allowed the government to pursue preferred economic policies without giving up control over the economy. Food subsidies as a significant feature of government policy, however, only became important in the 1970s, during the presidency of Anwar Sadat. The cost of wheat on international markets had increased and the value of the Egyptian pound had decreased. In addition, the government had become committed in both urban and rural areas to ensuring that Egyptians had enough to eat. Contemporary researchers argued that the major section of the population that concerned the state was the urban work force, whose wage demands had been circumvented by the subsidization:

> *The reluctance of the Government to remove or reduce the wheat subsidy is not centered so much on the likely effects on consumption levels as on the perceived hardship of the necessary price adjustment and the resulting wage demands by labor and Government workers. Removing the wheat subsidy would be equivalent to reducing real incomes by 4 percent.* (Blue et al. 1983:17)

Imported wheat allowed the government to subsidize bread in the cities and flour in the countryside. It is common to refer to an authoritarian bargain initially struck by Nasser in which the government exchanged guarantees of basic consumption for popular acquiescence in authoritarianism. The economic cost of the bargain did not weigh heavily on government finances until after Nasser's death.

In a celebrated 1991 article, "America's Egypt," Timothy Mitchell addressed the issue of subsidized food and asked, "Why has the country had to import ever increasing amounts of food?" (20). Mitchell's argument that Egyptians suffered from income inequality and too much spending on the military is a useful reminder of the real problems in Egypt. Mitchell's own preference, however, for what in Egyptian policy circles has long been known as 'food security' led him to some spectacular lapses. Mitchell believed that grain imports were driven primarily by the demand for meat and thus that the grain served as animal feed. On the contrary, wheat imports, the most important single food purchased on international markets, were for human consumption, while maize imports were indeed largely for animals. Mitchell appears to have viewed the increased cost and magnitude of wheat imports as a malign policy forced on Egyptians by the US government and their own to trap the country in a dependent relationship. Thus he argued that "in the subsequent oil boom years, income growth, together with massive US and Egyptian government subsidies, encouraged a broader switch from legumes and maize (corn) to less healthy diets of wheat and meat products" (Mitchell 1991:21). Responding to Mitchell's critique of development policies and their dietary effects, Alan Richards noted the association of maize with pellagra and proposed that "everywhere in the world where people are offered a choice between maize (or sorghum or cassava) and wheat bread, they choose the latter—if they can afford it" (Richards 1992:2, 43–45). This is no more true than Mitchell's assertion that maize and lentils are inherently healthier than wheat and meat. In Mexico maize remains the dominant grain and the primary foodstuff, where it is chosen by Mexicans as freely as any marketed food can be said to be. As they have for thousands of years, Mexicans continue to eat maize as their primary grain and pellagra is not a significant health problem. Parenthetically, the bioavailability of iron in maize is also low and "overreliance on maize has contributed to a high rate of iron deficiency" where it is a staple (Beiseigel et al. 2007:389). Wheat contains more iron (and more bioavailable iron) than maize, although whether it can provide sufficient iron without supplementation is an empirical question (Barrett and Ranum 1985:77–78).

The Mitchell–Richards interchange shows that thinking of foodstuffs as discrete dietary items is as attractively commonsensical as it is misleading. Maize is not inherently more or less healthy than wheat. The significant health problem associated with maize in the eighteenth and nineteenth centuries was the result of the way in which a particular technology interacted with a particular social and economic setting. Because we no longer live in the Garden of Eden where food offers itself up to us, most foodstuffs, but especially grains and animal protein, require processing to be edible. Their consumption is therefore embedded in a particular technology. In Europe, Africa, and the Middle East, maize was removed from the technology by which it was originally processed and embedded in a different one that, while familiar to the inhabitants, was poorly suited to making its nutritional value available. Placing maize back into its original New World food technology was one way to have avoided pellagra in the Old World as well as in those parts of the United States where slavery had been practiced.

It is therefore a useful thought experiment to consider replacing the *arepa*-like maize bread that many Egyptian peasants ate with tortillas. The thought experiment is not about Egyptian dietary habits but about ourselves. Rather than considering how to convince Egyptians to adopt the tortilla, let us consider our own reactions as scholars and researchers: why we are likely to think this is improbable, absurd, or impossible. If we do, it is most likely because we believe that tastes do not change rapidly or that the adoption of new foods is difficult or that the technology was alien. Perhaps it was because the necessary technology was embedded in women's labor and we have trouble considering their work as profoundly valuable to the task of ending hunger and disease.

It is unlikely the republican government led by army officers either in the Nasser era or under Sadat engaged in such thought experiments. Wheat is, as Richards may have meant to suggest, a higher-status food in Egypt precisely because it was associated with urban living, and with wealthier Egyptians in the countryside. Given its availability at concessional prices in the 1960s and at low prices for many periods during the ensuing five decades, it was an easy choice to make to ensure the authoritarian bargain that so many authors discuss as the basis of the regime's strength. Wheat promised to end both hunger and pellagra; in the process it would also, the government hoped, cement its hold on power.

By the 1970s wheat had largely replaced maize in Egyptian diets and the danger of pellagra was indeed eliminated. It was already apparent that Egyptians might soon be threatened by diabetes, something that has indeed occurred. The rise of obesity and diabetes can be associated to the increased consumption of highly refined flour (and sugar) just as the rise of pellagra was associated with the consumption of maize. Egypt today has one of the highest rates of diabetes in the world.[14] Nearly 17 percent of Egyptians have Type II diabetes and more than 86,000 Egyptians die every year from its effects. It has the seventeenth-highest prevalence of Type II diabetes globally.[15]

Here it seems we are led back to ask whether some foods are inherently less healthy than others, or perhaps why people choose to eat less healthy foods. Or we might wonder whether the experts who have shaped Egypt's food policies have malign intentions or, at best, so poorly understand the consequences of their decisions as to deserve to be stripped of all authority. We can get more traction in understanding the role of nutrition-based diseases, however, by stepping back a bit and recalling the history of Ireland in the mid nineteenth century and India in the twentieth.

Not unlike pellagra, the Great Famine (also known as the Great Hunger and the Irish Potato Famine) was also, fortuitously, the result of the interaction of a New World food technology with Old World social conditions. Potatoes provide less food energy than an equal weight of maize or wheat, but they are prolific and tolerant of the conditions in which they grow. They therefore provide more energy per

---

14 Mexico also has high rates of diabetes, which suggests that even diets high in nixtamalized corn are not necessarily healthier than those high in wheat products.

15 http:healthintelligence.drupalgardens.com/content/prevalence-diabetes-world-2013. The underlying data source is the IDF Diabetes Atlas (International Diabetes Foundation).

unit of area than maize or wheat. As with maize, Europeans deployed a fraction of the technology of potato production that was available in the New World. Specifically, a very limited number of genetic varieties of potatoes came to the Old World during the Columbian Exchange. In Ireland, tenant farmers were extremely economically insecure and impoverished and increasingly grew only one type. By the mid nineteenth century, potatoes, which had earlier been a supplementary food, became the primary food for most of the Irish. Although Ireland produced other food items such as beef, butter, and grain, these were exported to Britain. Low genetic variability made the potato crop especially vulnerable to disease, and in 1845 the first of a series of blights destroyed the potato harvest. By 1850 Ireland had lost some 1.5 million people due to death and emigration.

Two paths to avoid the famine were open to the British government. It chose neither. One would have been to close the country's ports and retain commodities that were exported to British markets for local consumption. The other would have been to initiate a significant public-works and relief program to allow the Irish population to buy food. What is now well understood is that the root of the Irish famine was not the lack of food but the lack of money with which to buy food. Local consumers could not compete with the prices British consumers would pay. Thus either local prices had to drop (through closing the export market) or local wages had to rise.

The fundamental problem for the Irish was their extreme reliance on a single foodstuff. The primary cause of this reliance was the search for the highest possible caloric intake consistent with their limited incomes. What maize was for Egyptian peasants in the late nineteenth and early twentieth centuries, potatoes were for the Irish in the nineteenth: a cheap source of calories. In both Egypt and Ireland, those who worked on the land could not necessarily retain (or, in the words of economists, did not choose to retain) goods that they produced. Higher-value Irish foods were sold and transported away; in Egypt, peasants, at least in the Delta, usually sold wheat they produced to urban residents who would pay more for it.

In 1981 Amartya Sen published the first of several works on famine. In it he made the point that famines do not occur because food is unavailable but because many laborers cannot afford to buy food. Sen proposed that the provision of public works to employ laborers would enable them to buy food and thus end the danger of famine.[16] What is also clear from work done after Sen's seminal publications is that even if it is possible to avert famine, there is no reason to believe that any particular kind of government intervention can avert malnutrition. What we do know is that poor people buy as many calories as they can with their money or their labor and that is almost invariably in the form of coarse grains. Only as their income (however broadly defined) increases do they shift to purchasing more expensive calories (such as higher-quality grains, animal products, or fruits) (Subramanian and Deaton 1996:154).

Egypt's wheat subsidy is a significant budget expenditure, although it is well understood that energy subsidies are a far larger drain on the budget. There is also no doubt that the wheat subsidy is not well targeted, although its allocation has improved significantly in the last 20 years. There are many arguments about whether Egypt, a country with large agricultural resources, should become self-sufficient in food production. Some of these arguments are grounded in abstract economic arguments, but many seem to be of the form that a country with so much available farmland has a kind of moral obligation to feed itself. In this chapter I have tried to look at how the Egyptian economy and society functioned when Egypt and Egyptians were almost entirely self-sufficient in food. Before the Second World War self-sufficiency in food production was acquired at the price of significant costs in nutrition for a large fraction of the population. This was most apparent in the form of pellagra and its attendant morbidity and mortality. The move to subsidized wheat and wheat flour benefited not only the urban population but the rural population as well. Those who wish to return to a world of self-sufficiency need to consider how they would ensure that the negative effects of self-sufficiency do not recur.

Although it is tempting to imagine Egyptian peasants living healthy lives with high levels of nutrition from their own production and perhaps producing a sufficient surplus to provide for the much larger

---

16 In later work Sen argued that the nature of state institutions also matters and that democracies will not suffer famine. Because Egypt has not had a famine in the twentieth century and because it is not a democracy, these later arguments by Sen are not relevant.

(absolutely and relatively) urban population today, this seems implausible to me. Far more important will be ways to enhance incomes.

References

Alderman, H., J. von Braun, and S. A. Sakr. 1982. *Egypt's Food Subsidy and Rationing System: A Description*. IFPRI Report No. 34. Washington, D.C.: International Food Policy Research Institute.

Alessandrini, G., and A. Scala. 1916. *Pellagra*. Part 1, *A New Contribution to the Etiology and Pathogenesis of Pellagra*, trans. E. M. Perdue; Part 2, *Pellagra in the United States*, by E. M. Perdue. Kansas City, MO: Burton Publishing Co.

Ayrout, H. H. 2005. *The Egyptian Peasant*, trans. John Alden. Cairo: American University in Cairo Press.

Barois, J. 1889. *Irrigation in Egypt*, trans. A. M. Miller. Washington: Government Printing Office.

Barrett, F., and P. Ranum. 1985. "Wheat Flour and Other Cereal-based Products." In F. M. Clydesdale and K. L. Wiemer, eds., *Iron Fortification of Foods*, 75–108. Orlando, FL: Academic Press.

Beiseigel, J. M., et al. 2007. "Iron Bioavailability from Maize and Beans: A Comparison of Human Measurements with Caco-2 Cell and Algorithm Predictions 1,2,3,4," *American Journal of Clinical Nutrition*, 86(2), August: 388–396.

Blue, R., et al. 1983. *PL 480 Title I: The Egyptian Case*. AID Project Impact Evaluation Report No. 45. Washington, DC: USAID.

Commonwealth Economic Committee. 1965. *Grain Crops*. London: Her Majesty's Stationery Office.

Cuno, K. 1992. *The Pasha's Peasants*. Cambridge, UK: Cambridge University Press.

FAO (Food and Agriculture Organization of the United Nations). 1992. "Maize in Human Nutrition." http://www.fao.org/docrep/t0395e/T0395E00.htm#Contents.

Folch, C. 2010. "Stimulating Consumption: Yerba Mate Myths, Markets and Meanings from Conquest to Present," *Comparative Studies in Society and History*, 52(1): 6–36.

Galal, O. M. 2002. "The Nutrition Transition in Egypt: Obesity, Undernutrition and the Food Consumption Context," *Public Health Nutrition*, 5(1A): 141–148.

Goldberg, E. 2006. "The Historiography of Crisis in the Egyptian Political Economy." In I. Gershoni, A. Singer, and Y. H. Erdem, eds., *Middle East Historiographies: Narrating the Twentieth Century*, 183–207. Berkeley: University of California Press.

Hansen, B. 1991. *Egypt and Turkey*. Oxford: Oxford University Press.

Harik, I. 1992. "Subsidization Policies in Egypt: Neither Economic Growth nor Distribution," *International Journal of Middle East Studies*, 24(3), August: 481–499.

Issawi, C. 1947. *Egypt: An Economic and Social Analysis*. Oxford: Oxford University Press.

Mariani-Costantini, R., and A. Mariani-Costantini. 2007. "An Outline of the History of Pellagra in Italy," *Journal of Anthropological Sciences*, 85: 163–171.

Mitchell, T. 1991. "America's Egypt," *Middle East Report*, 169, March–April: 18–34, 36.

Patwardhan, V. N., and W. J. Darby. 1972. *The State of Nutrition in the Arab Middle East*. Nashville, TN: Vanderbilt University Press.

Pearson, R. W. J. 1914. "Pellagrous Insanity in Egypt," *Transactions of the National Association for the Study of Pellagra*, 203–208. Columbia, SC: The R.L. Bryan Company.

"Pellagra in Egypt." 1920. *Journal of the American Medical Association*, 75(5): 321.

Perdue. 1916. *Pellagra in the United States*. Part 2 of G. Alessandrini and A. Scala, *Pellagra*. MO: Burton Publishing Co.

Reber, E. A. 2006. "A Hard Row to Hoe: Changing Maize Use in the American Bottom and Surrounding Areas." In J. E. Staller, R. H. Tykot, and B. F. Benz, eds., *Histories of Maize: Multidisciplinary Approaches to the Prehistory, Linguistics, Biogeography, Domestication, and Evolution of Maize*, 236–248. Amsterdam: Elsevier Press.

Richards, A. 1982. *Egypt's Agricultural Development, 1800–1980: Technical and Social Change*. Boulder, CO: Westview Press.

———. 1992. "America's Egypt: A Flawed Critique," *Middle East Report*, 174, Jan.–Feb.: 2, 43–45.

Roberts, S. R. 1914. *Pellagra*. St. Louis: C. V. Mosby Company.

Ross, M. A. 1956. "Nutrition and Home-economics Programme in Egyptian Villages," *Proceedings of the Nutrition Society*, 15(1) March: 30–35.

References

Sandwith, F. M. 1915. "Pellagra Considered from the Point of View of a Disease of Insufficient Nutrition," *Transactions of the Society of Tropical Medicine and Hygiene*, 9(1) October: 1–15.

Schwarcz, H. P. 2006. "Stable Carbon Isotope Analysis and Human Diet: A Synthesis." In J. E. Staller, R. H. Tykot, and B. F. Benz, eds., *Histories of Maize: Multidisciplinary Approaches to the Prehistory, Linguistics, Biogeography, Domestication, and Evolution of Maize*, 315–324. Amsterdam: Elsevier.

Subramanian, S., and A. Deaton. 1996. "The Demand for Food and Calories," *Journal of Political Economy*, 104(1) February: 133–162.

Young, V. R., and P. L. Pellett. 1985. "Wheat Proteins in Relation to Protein Requirements and Availability of Amino Acids," *American Journal of Clinical Nutrition*, 41(5 supp) May: 1077–1090.

CHAPTER 4

Where Is Our *Baladi* Food?

Sara Pozzi and Sara El Sayed

Introduction

> *Food Sovereignty is the right of people to healthy and culturally appropriate food produced through ecologically sound and sustainable methods, and their right to define their own food and agriculture systems.* (Rosset 2003:1)

La Via Campesina, the international movement founded in 1993 by peasant organizations of small and middle-scale producers from Latin America, Asia, North America, Africa, and Europe, points to food sovereignty as a method of achieving local development in rural areas. Specifically, this is done through the creation of "local circuits of productions and consumptions" (Rosset 2003:1).

The first section of this chapter will assess the consequences of agricultural development policies in Egypt over the past 30 years and how those policies have impacted Egyptian food production and the lives of food producers. We will attempt in particular to measure these issues against the principle of food sovereignty. The second section will describe a specific attempt to promote food sovereignty values within local Egyptian communities. We will explore the non-governmental organization Nawaya and its food arm Baladini, which together spearhead initiatives aimed at creating systemic change to the food production system in order to safeguard Egyptian sociocultural and environmental ecosystems.

The People's Right to "Food Produced through Ecologically Sound and Sustainable Methods"

Egypt remains a predominantly agricultural country, with its development depending primarily on rural resources. As stated by Shalaby et al., "Agriculture contributes approximately 14% of the GDP and absorbs about 31% of workforce. About 53% population lives in rural areas where directly or indirectly their livelihood depends upon the agricultural sector" (2011:581). And yet, as of 2014 Egypt was a net importer of food, with estimates pointing at a foreign dependence of 60 percent for grains, sugar, meat, and edible oils. As Daniel Pipes states, "Egypt imports two-thirds of its wheat (10 million tons of a total of 15 million, making it the world's largest importer of wheat), 70 percent of its beans, and 99 percent of its lentils."[1] The alarming size of these numbers raises serious questions about the future sustainability of the food system in Egypt.

This chapter seeks to support the claim that moving toward local food production, with food-producing families as the basis of local and national economic development, should be taken into serious consideration by policy makers. To begin, we will briefly reflect on how the country ended up with such distressing figures, as well as the consequences on the micro level. In other words, how do the macro figures presented above reflect the reality of smallholder farmers as producers and consumers? What effects did post-Nasser policies have on the quality of life and rights for smallholder communities? Do people have access to "food produced through ecologically sound and sustainable methods" (Rosset 2003:1)?

The greatest challenges in modern rural Egypt began as neoliberal-oriented policies were promoted in the 1980s. Specifically, this was seen through the liberalization of the agricultural market, especially inputs, products, and land. Those policies culminated with the 1992/1996 law that changed the rules for renting land, removed price controls over land, and gave the landowner the ability to unilaterally terminate contracts with tenants (Saad 2004). This set of policies was overtly directed at benefiting landowners holding more than 50 feddans, as well as promoting large agribusiness investments for export. Currently, 80 percent of all Egyptian landowners own five feddans or less (Kruseman and Vullings 2007).

---

1 Daniel Pipes, "Hunger Growls in Egypt," *The Washington Times*, October 6, 2014, www.danielpipes.org/14989/egypt-hunger

Among the many adverse effects that the new land reforms accrued for smallholders, in particular we highlight the decreased capacity for household self-provisioning: "The first point to make is the growing dependence many households seem to have upon the market for providing access to foodstuffs and inputs for crop sales" (Bush 1999:107). For the smallholder farmer, often the only choice at the end of the season is to sell the entire harvest on the market. Paradoxically, after a season of hard work on their land, many rural families end up buying food for their own consumption at higher prices and lower quality from local markets.

The sale of the harvest is done in part to repay debt contracted with the middleman, who normally pays for inputs (such as seeds and fertilizer) at the beginning of the season. To clarify, the middleman is often a well-connected individual within rural regions who is in a position to distribute much-needed cash to farmers, covering the cost of inputs at the start of each agricultural season. At the end of the season, the same individual often cuts deals with wholesalers and outlets to purchase and sell the agricultural production. From Bush's investigations we read:

There has been considerable disquiet regarding profiteering by middlemen who have taken advantage of market liberalization and increased prices of inputs for peasant producers. The increase in input prices has not been offset by revenue for farm households that have insufficient land to generate sales of high market value or that are without access to alternative sources of cash to cover essential purchases. (Bush 1999:130)

This new kind of transaction seems to be common practice across the Egyptian rural landscape. Farmers from Qalyubiya and Dumyat governorates echo the concerns of many rural households Nawaya have been working with. Bush notes that as a result of this uniform liberalization strategy, rather than adequately addressing agricultural modernization it instead conflates power struggles, as "relatively new and unhindered power brokers in the village becomes a main issue for land-less and poorer members of the sample—not surprisingly as the larger landholders have started to usurp the roles of providers of inputs (and employers of labour) that were previously preformed by the hitherto much maligned cooperative" (1999:130).

"Sustainable and sound methods" of food production were not crucial to the reformed agriculture policies. Over the past 30 years, Egypt has faced a progressive erosion of natural resources, particularly water and soil. This has been aggravated by inappropriate agricultural practices.

Concerning pesticides and fertilizers, for example, while removing state subsidies was thought of as a means for discouraging their usage, evidence shows that "the application of these two inputs has not uniformly declined and that the deterioration in their quality since the liberalization has meant that farmers have had to apply more of these chemically based compounds with less effect on productivity and possibly more detrimental effect on the environment" (Bush 1999:125). Regarding the level and quality of irrigation water, major issues are connected with land reclamation projects and new channels being dug. Water pollution, meanwhile, derives mostly from discharging poultry waste in the canals, the decreasing movement of silt connected with the high dam, and poor drainage systems that have increased groundwater level, its salinity, and consequently the salinity of soil (Bush 1999).

In addition, Bush indicates a general sense of disenfranchisement of farmers from their land as a consequence of the practices of dispossession caused by the law:

> *The third major effect of the land law was that tenants did not see much reason for trying to preserve the quality of the land that they were farming if it was likely that might be dispossessed within two years. The farmers were, in their words, waiting to see what was going to happen and they were unlikely and unwilling to invest in the land if they were no longer going to be guaranteed rights to it. That meant an obvious reluctance to invest in drainage and other environmentally important projects.* (Bush 1999:118)

Transfer of new knowledge and techniques in agriculture from the government through extension programs has been limited and, most importantly, does not always reach smallholder farmers. These farmers are thus unable to face the challenges in an environment that has changed so rapidly (Shalaby et al. 2011).

As noted by Bush:

Villagers were also looking for a lead from government in helping raise the productivity of land and help with extension services. But this would have to be a universal service and not one directed only to wealthier families, as seems to have been the case in the past, when the politics of patronage and local connections seemed to shape the allocation of common resources like extension and cooperative services. (Bush 1999:131)

The picture for the small-scale food producer is also bleak. In the wake of global neoliberal trends, Egyptian policies have led to the uneven concentration of Egyptian agribusiness and capital: "the country's top six companies account for 41 per cent of the country's total value of exports, driven by EFG Hermes and links to Citadel Capital, PICO and Americana" (Bush 2016:168). In such contexts, the small-scale business of adding value to crops by transforming them into processed food can be technically and legally challenging. Small-scale food producers often lack access to streams of capital, information, or equipment. Information on food technologies for small to middle-sized agro-businesses, for example, can be difficult to access through government offices or chambers of commerce. Economically, most equipment that is readily available in the country is tailored for large-scale food industries; small-scale technologies for local food production are few and far between.

The People's Right to "Healthy and Culturally Appropriate Food"
Owning small plots of land on which they make a living, and often at the whims of middlemen, smallholder farmers struggle to provide the necessities of food, education, and health care. Family budgets in rural areas across the country are tight, and as a result many families are forced to purchase the cheap, processed food and drinks available at local village corners. Most of these options are "low-nutrition [and] calorie-dense, causing both nutritional deficiencies and obesity" (Pipes 2014). This pattern of consumption is also encouraged by television and advertisements that promote a "modern," "fast," and "consumerist" way of living and eating, contributing to a shift away from traditional food-making habits. These

trends have not only contributed to increased stunting due to malnutrition among Egyptian children—31 percent of Egyptian children between six months and five years of age are malnourished, one of the highest rates in the world—but also affect the entire adult population, with 5.2 percent of Egyptians going hungry (CAPMAS, cited in Pipes 2014).

Nawaya was an initiative that sought to improve livelihoods for rural farming communities in Egypt. Inspired by the definition of food sovereignty and supported by the ideal of preserving agro-biodiversity throughout Egypt, Nawaya began collaborating with rural communities in the Badrashin area of the Giza governorate, on the outskirts of Cairo. Sadly, the team's conversations in 2011 with rural families in this region mirrored the realities described above.

The Nawaya initiative began its work by protecting and bringing back indigenous inputs and breeds, as well as introducing innovative ecological farming practices. Combining different frameworks, Nawaya connected with existing extension services in Egypt while deriving inspiration from innovative methods to create sustainable ways of living in rural areas, such as permaculture and biodynamic agriculture. Nawaya's work with the farmers on making chemical-free compost to sell on the market, preserving indigenous breeds such as the Bigawi chicken, and upholding raw honey traditions raised issues of access to high-quality food for the communities themselves and the loss of traditional food-processing knowledge.

As a result of these conversations, the constraints faced by the farmers in providing high-quality, nutritious food for their families, and especially for their children, were clearly defined. The team explored questions such as: How does a young mother decide which food to prepare for her family? What decision-making power does she have when she needs to take into consideration the frugality dictated by scarcity, the time constraints dictated by the necessity to help generate income for the household, and the easy availability, in rural communities, of cheap processed food that can be purchased on the way to school or work?

Going *Baladi*: "The Right to Define Their Own Food and Agriculture Systems"

The initial work of Nawaya required redefining, preserving, protecting, and diffusing local varieties of seeds and breeds within rural communities. But Nawaya came to understand that in order to safeguard endangered food more broadly and sustainably, its work needed to connect with a wider public of consumers, food makers, and supporters who were able to appreciate and spread the values of preserving and valorizing food traditions and indigenous products.

It was at this stage that a group of rural Egyptian women played a particularly relevant role in leading Nawaya toward the creation of its food arm, Baladini. Nawaya saw rural women as the guardians of food traditions in Egypt. As Saad and Ayeb affirmed in their study, "women have in time contributed to conservation and management of the natural resources needed for basic survival and food security of their communities" (Ayeb and Saad 2009:131). In conversations with the Nawaya team, a small, multi-generational group of women from Saqqara fervently expressed the necessity of keeping good food-making practices alive. They pointed to lost food traditions with disappointment, agreeing with Wassef that "recent decades have witnessed the progressive erosion of the traditional Egyptian diet and the introduction of new foods and eating habits" (Wassef 2004:1). The women strongly supported the idea of bringing back these traditions.

This concept of traditional, or *baladi*,[2] food resonates in many conversations with food producers. Ayeb and Saad have helped to define *baladi* in the literature: "[it] literally means 'of the country'... it denotes that which is local or home-bred in opposition to foreign or imported object or produce. In agriculture it is synonym with local varieties of both plant and animal products" (2009:139). The birth of Baladini—a wordplay on the *baladi* concept—resulted organically from these initial conversations and relationships between the Nawaya team and Badrashin women. A small group of women felt the need to reflect and act to preserve the value of indigenous food and *baladi* traditions. In a way, Baladini was a concrete answer to the question posed by the third part of the food-sovereignty definition: "the right to define their own food and agriculture systems." When the women first came together, they began to produce traditional food products and sell them at farmers' markets in urban Cairo. Through this process, they began to ask

---

2 Distinguishing it from its possible 'nationalistic' connotation, we will use the terms *baladi*, 'local,' and 'indigenous' food in this chapter to refer to the ecologically appropriate and biodiverse food patrimony of the various Egyptian ecosystems.

questions related to food production. What kind of food makes sense in a specific environment and why? What are the benefits of consuming indigenous food rather than ready-to-go processed ones? How can they make *baladi* food appeal to a wider public, and particularly younger, less aware generations?

It is important at this point to mention the efforts of the Slow Food network, which acted as a font of inspiration and helped construct Baladini's identity in the early period. Slow Food actively contributes to the collection and spreading of indigenous food knowledge across the globe. To support people reflecting on the "right to define their own food and agriculture systems" and fighting to preserve endangered breeds, seeds, and food practices, Slow Food built the Ark of Taste project. The Ark of Taste is "an online catalogue that is growing day by day, gathering alerts from people who see the flavors of their childhood disappear, taking with them a piece of the culture and history of which they are a part."[3] Thanks to the Ark of Taste's efforts in traveling the world "to collect small-scale quality productions that belong to the cultures, history and traditions of the entire planet and that risk to go extinct within a few generations," Egyptians from all over the country, including the participants in Baladini, were offered opportunities to rediscover and protect their indigenous food. So far, 20 endangered indigenous foods and breeds have been identified in different categories, including breads (*merahrah* bread, *fayesh* bread, *zallut* bread, *shamsi* bread), spices and teas (*habak* [horsemint], *bardaqush* [Egyptian sage], *za'tar* [wild majoram], *bu'aytharan* [wormwood], *rabl'* [ladies' false fleabane]), dairy products (*mish* cheese, *gameed*, *zebda baladi*, *samn baladi*), Siwa salt, Bigawi chicken, the Egyptian honeybee, and *fesikh*.

Good, Clean, and Healthy Food as Model for Change: What Is Baladini?

What began as a project producing handmade pasta using Nawaya eggs and local wheat has since expanded to a rural, woman-led, farm-to-fork kitchen focusing on the processing of healthy grains sourced from local farmers. An educational component integrated into everyday activities is integral to the business since Baladini recognizes the need to broaden,

---

3 Slow Food website: http://www.fondazioneslowfood.com/en/what-we-do/the-ark-of-taste/about-the-project/

systematize, and document collective food knowledge and business practices in order to be better able to produce high-quality food.

Toward the end of the first year of its work, Baladini brought together the women who had participated in the project to collectively define the initiative. What came out of the workshop was: "Baladini is a women's food project that develops rural food through cooperation and education." When explaining the project to an outsider the group often offers a visual image: a team of women working on revitalizing and reinventing Egyptian *baladi* food traditions, making *akl mudallah*, or 'food with a light woman's touch.' The food products that Baladini offers were often born as variants of products rooted in rural food-making traditions—a new spice, a new shape, a novel conservation technique. The final products often reflected the rich biodiversity of the area where Baladini works and the competencies of women passed on from generation to generation.

To constantly innovate and enrich its food lines, a core team in Baladini researches the sociobiological characteristics of the products, considering where the main ingredients are sourced in the area, examining the quality of the raw ingredients, deconstructing traditional processing practices, and sometimes innovating or adding to the original recipe. This was the case for one of Baladini's currently most popular products, *'aish bettaw bi-l-kharob*. Carob is a highly nutritious fruit with a long history in Egypt, but has become largely forgotten in the current Egyptian diet. A team of Baladini women explored the fruit together, and by transforming it into a flour and adding it to the dough of the traditional *bettaw* bread—a fenugreek corn bread that had been made for millennia in Upper Egypt—the top-selling product of Baladini was born. By adding carob to the bread, the team created a unique fusion, a sweet and savory cracker with special nutritional components. This product, along with many other 'reinvented' foods, is sold at farmers' markets and small stores in Cairo, primarily within networks of individuals aware of the food issues encompassed in Baladini's mission.

By revitalizing old food processing practices and techniques and sharing them with urban and farming communities, Baladini women seek to preserve *baladi* traditions, connect rural and urban communities across and beyond Egypt, break barriers of mistrust between them, and reappropriate forgotten knowledge and practices. In addition, this process of making and selling *baladi* food can be a way for Egyptian women to push for change in different socioeconomic fields: better human health, increased access to diverse, tasty, and nutritious food, heightened awareness of the biodiversity of Egyptian products and breeds, deepened human relationships to local food practices, and promotion of the roles of women and farmers, their knowledge, and their contribution to society.

A Small, Inclusive Business: Challenges for the Years to Come

Baladini, initially supported by start-up/development funds, is attempting to transition toward financial sustainability through its business lines. The hope is that the model will cover both operational and educational activities. While navigating this transitional phase, we envision the project transforming gradually into what we can label, following the newest paradigm of development, an 'inclusive business' (sometimes also referred to in academia as a social business/entrepreneurship venture). The novelty of the model is defined primarily by "the primacy of social benefit, what Duke University professor Greg Dees in his seminal work on the field characterizes as the pursuit of 'mission-related impact'" (Martin and Osberg 2007:9).

During its first two years of operation, Baladini sought to equip rural women to lead their own artisanal food businesses based on the production and sale of rural foods through a series of on-the-job mentorships ('mission-related impact'). In the ensuing years, the program will aim to place the entire food production chain—growing, production, processing, sale, and marketing of food—in the hands of farming communities. The goal will be to increase local family incomes, while simultaneously valorizing rural work for its contribution to society. In doing so, Baladini is a pioneer in Egypt—a small-scale, artisanal business that is experimenting with different paths to inclusiveness by testing and implementing various organizational, management, and financial models.

The challenge over the years to come will be to harness the most creative and anarchic aspects of food making, valorize rural knowledge, include rural women in every aspect of the business (operational management, product development, and strategic planning), give primacy to the relationships and people participating in it and to their communities, and build the start-up business to the point of sustainability. A primary question in this effort will be how to reconcile in practice the necessity to be competitive and efficient ('competitive advantage' in the literature) with the 'relational value,' defined by Elyachar as "value produced in workshop exchanges ... since it expresses the positive value attached to the creation, reproduction, and extension of the relationships in communities of Cairo" (Elyachar 2005:7).

From Homemade to Artisanal: An Alternative Turn for the Food Movement in Egypt

While questioning these levels of complexity and without any pretense of having any set solutions at this stage, a possible direction that can inspire others to join the experiment is contextualizing Baladini as a production space that marks the passage from homemade to artisanal. The Nawaya/Baladini teams are exploring this as a possible solution for many rural communities to escape the circle of forced marginalization.

'Artisanal' products are those that are "homemade, handcrafted from natural ingredients, personalized, simplified, local, and rich with taste. Some observers have identified the growing interest in artisanal food as the Slow Food Movement because the growth, production and sales are done in low-technology, local and simplified ways" (Hess 2009:ix). In Baladini's values manifesto, artisanal is celebrated by the beauty of small. It means knowing your ingredients, conditions, and seasons, and making your recipes with care. Emphasis is placed on indigenous foods and traditional processing techniques that maintain nutritional value. Ingredients [are] sourced from farmers employing natural growing methods. Baladini also emphasizes that people and the environment are at the center of food exchange: artisanal implies good prices for producer and consumer bounded in a local circle of knowledge about food and its processing techniques. It promotes respect for diversity, working together collaboratively, and the development of inclusive economies (www.baladini.com).

In addition to setting a precedent by seeking to foster the development of local artisanal food businesses that could be replicated by other rural communities outside the confines of its production space, Baladini is also seeking to foster new inclusive markets characterized by a particular cluster of values (collaboration and shared interests, social and environmental fairness, valorizing local resources, and producer–consumer relationships). In the long term, the result would be a diverse and integrated community of farmers, producers, project staff, consumers, and volunteers exchanging goods, knowledge, and practices, who could also together advocate for the creation of fairer and more inclusive markets and policies.

We are currently seeing the fruits of these activities through a small success taking place among artisanal producers in Cairo. In partnership with the Slow Food Cairo chapter, a group of producers have come together to develop a preliminary set of guidelines that would be fair for the producer, the vendor, and the consumer. The guidelines aim to combine good business sense with values-based markets, setting some ground rules about where to rebuild food markets and establishing a precedent for small vendors to negotiate space for interacting with customers, fair prices, marketing modalities, learning platforms, and developing other tools to benefit the collective.

The challenges awaiting the artisanal network in Egypt are enormous. A recent UNIDO report emphasizes the problematic of a sector characterized by business informality and lack of innovation:

Micro, Small and Medium Enterprises (MSMEs) comprise over 97% of private enterprises in Egypt and account for 85% of non-agricultural private sector employment and almost 40% of total employment. Over 80% of MSMEs are informal, and characterised by low value-added and low production quality. In order to improve the national industrial competitiveness, it is required to overcome impediments to trade, provide demand-driven technical training, facilitate efficiency improvements and provide institutional capacity building to support institutions. (2013:9)

Indeed, the Baladini team has experienced these constraints in its everyday operational activities. To highlight a few of the most prominent issues, first, Baladini producers must be accountable for the cleanliness of the products offered. This is an enormous responsibility considering the ecological disaster[4] of the agricultural system. Traceability and storage of raw materials constitute a real challenge and often

---

4 As noted by Dasgupta it is the complexity of the "resource allocation mechanisms which do not take advantage of dispersed information, which are insensitive to hidden (and often not-so-hidden) economic and ecological interactions…which do not take the long view, and which do not give a sufficiently large weight to the claims of the poorest within rural population (particularly women and children in these populations) [that] are going to prove environmentally disastrous" (Dasgupta in Bush 1999:156).

further complicate the food processing chain. Second, the lack of state-sponsored research, guides, and investment to develop an agro-business market for MSMEs forces artisanal businesses to find secondary solutions for surviving in the market and distributing their products while maintaining standards of hygiene and safety.

In addition, the Egyptian market lacks food equipment that can serve a small business, forcing small startups to get their equipment shipped from abroad at much higher costs. The Slow Food Network in Egypt portrays this through everyday examples, including importing a simple pressure canning machine from the US and commissioning equipment for vegetable and fruit solar drying from Germany.

Finally, in a sociopolitical climate where mistrust and corruption reign, it was and still is quite energy-intensive to form and keep alive a network of cooperative small businesses and customers who hold similar values and fight for a space on the food scene. They must constantly push legislators for better regulations and protection.

Concluding with Many Outstanding Questions

Returning to the question posed at the beginning of the chapter—"Where is our *baladi* food?"—the only answer we have at this point in time derives from the research and experiences of Nawaya, Slow Food, and other similar small initiatives. Much of the work has taken place within the past five years.

Many questions remain. What is Baladini really doing when it is reinventing and marketing *baladi* food traditions? What gets lost in those reinvention passages, and what is the socioeconomic impact of the loss? What kind of accountability can the business promise to the people and to their knowledge? How can we preserve local knowledge while transforming it as needed to meet business standards? How do we respect its essence?

Other questions concern the social implications and impact of the work of Baladini as a small business in terms of its business operations and strategies. Is Baladini situated among bottom-billion initiatives that are rebranding the transformative, inclusive power of entrepreneurship, inviting newly transformed subjects to "help [themselves] to a piece of the market" (Rajak 2008:317)? Does it seek to fix "gaps in the market," or does it fundamentally redress "inequities in the way markets function" (Meagher 2015:851)? What does 'doing business' entail within the Egyptian rural community where Baladini is located? Is capitalistic language, with its specific set of rules, systems, and mechanisms prioritized in the transactions of goods and services, already in use among rural communities? Or are market transactions among communities instead informed and directed by communities' relationships? And as the startup products begin to circulate within different markets, will Baladini be able both to expand and to remain socially and environmentally accountable (Blowfield and Dolan 2014:36)?

At another level, challenges face the strategies by which Baladini operates at the organizational level. What are the mechanisms that were successful in keeping the group together? Where is the organization failing and why? Is the project succeeding in allowing people from different backgrounds to work together, trust, and cooperate with each other? Or is the attempt just exacerbating mistrust within the unstable political and economic reality and highlighting the limitations of the development and the business worlds in which Baladini operates?

These questions cannot be answered at the moment. However, some positive indicators already suggest that, at a micro level, the model is contributing to improving the food consumption habits and food viability for rural and urban communities, as well as keeping the discussion alive on the necessity of a systemic change in agriculture.

As activists, the Nawaya group believes that, in order to safeguard indigenous food and food-making traditions, they need to reactivate a collaborative process among different segments of Egyptian society. The great biodiversity in Egypt is an opportunity to launch a network of small artisanal producers, contributing to local economies and to the well-being of a wider consumer audience. Much work awaits: identifying and documenting *baladi* artisanal products, setting healthy standards, ensuring access to equipment, and sensitizing the market, consumers, and government. But it is safe to say that, even if at a micro level, something is moving.

References

Ayeb, H., and R. Saad. 2009. "Gender, Poverty, and Agro-biodiversity Conservation in Rural Egypt and Tunisia." In H. Ayeb and R.

Saad, eds., *Agrarian Transformation in the Arab World: Persistent and Emerging Challenges, Cairo Papers in Social Science,* 32(2): 129–155.

Blowfield, M., and C. S. Dolan. 2014. "Business as a Development Agent: Evidence of Possibility and Improbability," *Third World Quarterly,* 35(1): 22–42.

Bush, R. 1999. *Economic Crisis and the Politics of Reform in Egypt.* Boulder, CO: Westview Press.

———. 2016. "Uprisings without Agrarian Questions." In Ali Kadri, ed., *Development Challenges and Solutions after the Arab Spring,* 153–174. Rethinking International Development Series. Basingstoke, UK: Palgrave Macmillan.

Elyachar, J. 2005. *Markets of Dispossession: NGOs, Economic Development, and the State in Cairo.* Durham, NC: Duke University Press.

Hess, L. 2009. *Artisanal Theology: Intentional Formation in Radically Covenantal Companionship.* Eugene, OR: Cascade.

Kruseman, G., and W. Vullings. 2007. "Rural Development Policy towards 2025: Targeted Conditional Income Support: A Suitable Option?" *Wageningen, Alterra, Alterra-rapport.* Available at: www.alterra.wur.nl.

Martin, R. L., and S. Osberg. 2007. "Social Entrepreneurship: The Case for Definition," *Stanford Social Innovation Review,* 11: 1–17.

Meagher, K. 2015. "Leaving No One Behind? Informal Economies, Economic Inclusion and Islamic Extremism in Nigeria," *Journal of International Development,* 27: 835–855.

Rajak, D. 2008. " 'Uplift and Empower': The Market, Morality, and Corporate Responsibility on South Africa's Platinum Belt." In Geert de Neve, ed., *Hidden Hands in the Market: Ethnographies of Fair Trade, Ethical Consumption, and Corporate Social Responsibility,* 297–324. Research in Economic Anthropology 28. Bingley, UK: Emerald JAI.

Rosset, P. 2003. "Food Sovereignty: Global Rallying Cry of Farmer Movements," *Food First,* 9(4): 1–3.

Saad, R. 2004. "Social and Political Costs of Coping with Poverty in Rural Egypt." Paper presented at the Fifth Mediterranean Social and Political Research Meeting, Florence and Montecatini, Terme 24–28 March, organized by the Mediterranean Programme of the Robert Schuman Centre for Advanced Studies at the European University Institute.

Shalaby, M. Y., K. H. al-Zahrani, M. B. Baig, G. S. Straquadine, and F. Aldosari. 2011. "Threats and Challenges to Sustainable Agriculture and Rural Development in Egypt: Implications for Agricultural Extension," *Journal of Animal and Plant Sciences*, 21(3): 581–588.

UNIDO, 2013. "UNIDO Activities in Egypt." http://www.undp.org.eg/Portals/0/z_UNDAF%202007_2011%20English.pdf

Wassef, H. 2004. "Food Habits of the Egyptians: Newly Emerging Trends," *Eastern Mediterranean Health Journal*, 10(6): 1–18.

CHAPTER 5

Agri-food System Dynamics in a South Lebanon Village, 1920–2015

Saker El Nour

Introduction: The Agriculture Sector in Lebanon

In the Middle East and North Africa (MENA), particularly in the Arab East, there has been over the last forty years a tremendous decline in food self-sufficiency and a consequent boom in food imports (Le Mouël et al. 2015).

Lebanon is considered a major food importer, with local production satisfying only 20% of domestic consumption. The country produces about 15% of its wheat consumption, meaning that the country is far from being self-sufficient in grain production and has to depend on imports (UNEP 2005). It also produces only 45% of its legumes and 10% of its sugar needs. It imports 78% of its dairy and meat products. However, it is self-sufficient in poultry production, and it exports fruits and vegetables, including apples, potatoes, citrus fruits, and tomatoes. Agricultural exports account for 19% of total exports. Nearly 99% of these exports are sent to Arab countries, with Saudi Arabia (22%), Kuwait (16%), and the United Arab Emirates (9%) as the top Gulf destination markets (Ministry of Agriculture 2014).

The Lebanese diet is considered the most 'westernized' nutritional system in the Middle East and North Africa region, that is, it is high in saturated fats and red meats (Le Mouël et al. 2015). While it is important to understand the agri-food system dynamics at all levels, this national 'big picture' does not give us any empirical evidence about the transformations that have occurred in the agri-food system at the household or village level.

With regard to the village agri-food system dynamics in a South Lebanon village, the key contribution of this chapter is to give attention to the local dynamics in national and international agri-food relations. It aims to provide a platform for discussions about changes in the agri-food system at the micro level. The village food system is viewed as the result of uneven development of global agri-food commodity structures. This perspective focuses attention on food producers and explains the variety of relationships at the community level.

Accordingly, the chapter proceeds as follows. The first section outlines elements of a conceptual framework for exploring possible links between political and economic context, livelihoods, and agri-food dynamics. This serves as a basis for the research questions that underlie the empirical analysis. The second section presents the contexts of the case study from South Lebanon, while the third analyzes the structures of food systems, and the transformations that have occurred in each historical period. The final section offers a discussion of the results, and suggests movement drivers that determine the trajectories of agri-food systems in the village.

Conceptual Framework and Research Questions

The food system is defined as a chain of activities connecting food production, processing, distribution, consumption, and waste management, as well as all the associated regulatory institutions and activities (Kaufman and Kameshwari 2000). The food system is driven within and influenced by both global and local forces (Goodman 1997). Cultural, political, natural, and economic systems shape the way we understand the interrelated core components of the food system.

Food-regime theory is based in part on Polanyi's (1957) analysis of capitalist transformation. Since the appearance of Harriet *Friedmann* and Philip *McMichael's* article in the journal *Sociologia Ruralis* in 1989, the food-regimes approach has been among the most influential framing tools in agri-food systems studies. *McMichael* has defined the food regime as "the historically specific geo-political-economic organization of international agricultural and food relations" (McMichael 2004: 3). *Friedmann* and *McMichael* identify two global food regimes so far: the first (1870–1914) during the period of British hegemony in the world economy, and the second (1945–1973) under US hegemony in the postwar world economy. In 2005 McMichael added a third food regime (1980s–2000s), called the "corporate food regime," under the Transnational Corporations (TNCs) of agriculture, and agro-exports (McMichael, 2005).

Some scholars have been critical, however, of food-regime and political-economy approaches in general for presenting an overly determinist portrayal of capitalist accumulation as a force of transformation in the agri-food system. This criticism challenges the legitimacy of assuming the coherence of food regimes over particular historical periods all over the world. In doing so, these critics contend, the food-regimes approach glosses over national and regional particularities of restructuring and political contestation. There is, however, a growing field of studies that takes a country or a region as a starting point for the analysis (e.g., Chinnakonda and Telford 2007; Thompson, Harper, and Kraus 2008). 'Local' and 'regional' food have come increasingly into focus in the media, academic writing, and the food-justice movement in western societies, as they are thought to provide environmental and economic benefits over 'global' or 'non-regional food' (e.g., Jablonski and Yuri 2012; Hinrichs 2000). A local food system refers to a system in which food is produced in a small from which it can be marketed directly to consumers (Haapanen 2011). There is no consensus on a definition in terms of the distance between production and consumption. For example, according to the definition adopted by the US Congress in the Food, Conservation, and Energy Act (2008 Farm Act), the total distance within which a product can be considered a "locally or regionally produced agricultural food product" is less than 400 miles (643 km) from its origin, or within the state in which it is produced (Martinez et al. 2013). Most food-movement activists, however, consider 'local' to be on a smaller scale than the state level. Some have reduced this distance to 100 miles (160 km). In addition to geographic proximity of producer and consumer, however, local food can also be defined in terms of socio-ecological and short-supply-chain characteristics. One of the lacunas of this approach is that the local food studies focus on alternative food chains rather than global–local relations. In addition, the main geographical focus of local food-system studies has been Western Europe and North America. This approach also neglects the agrarian class and changes in agricultural production. Contemporary agriculture, as Bernstein (2015) explains, is shaped by the historical development of a wide range of social-class and labor relationships and forms of agrarian capital formation.

A review of food-systems literature reveals few studies from the perspective of global south. Read and Jones (2002) have conceptualized a "village food system," which involves both subsistence foods and those traded from outside the village area. The local production consists of domestic crop-growing and livestock-keeping, and the output can be either sold to the market or consumed by the farming households themselves.

In this study we will develop a sociohistorical analysis of the dynamics of agri-food system in South Lebanon based on the framework developed by Haapanen (2011), Read and Jones (2002), Polanyi's concept of embeddedness in his seminal work *The Great Transformation* (1957), and finally the verification of the holistic perspective of the global food regime developed by Harriet Friedmann and Philip McMichael.

For Polanyi, economic embeddedness means that the economy is immersed in social relations and cannot be separated from society dynamics (Machado 2011). While Polanyi's work offers a macro-level historical explanation of the development of the nineteenth-century capitalist market economy, in this chapter we will use his framework to analyze agri-food embeddedness at the micro level—in other words, the embeddedness and/or disembeddedness of village agri-food in the local society.

While Read and Jones (2002:38) do not consider the hunter-gatherer as an internal part of the village food system, it is nevertheless appropriate to incorporate these activities into the analysis of this study. Hunting and especially gathering represent fundamental elements of village food security in the study area at certain specific times. In addition, food aid provided by political parties continues to have a significant place in rural South Lebanon (Love 2010). The combination of the 'village food system' approach and the 'global food regime' view aims to explain the interconnections between the micro and macro levels of food-regime dynamics. Our approach combining 'agriculture' and 'food' signals a focus on production and consumption, and the components of the food supply chain in between and around production and consumption. We address the social relations of agri-food production in its dynamics. This type of systems perspective recognizes that food markets, and the policies intended to influence these markets, are interconnected.

The key questions regarding the dynamics in the agri-food system that this study seeks to answer are: What are the changing dynamics in the patterns of production, circulation, and consumption of food in the village? What are the driving factors of these changes? In what ways are agricultural and food value chains being restructured, and who is benefiting the most from such restructuring? In what directions do the dynamics of Sinay diet systems move? What are the relations between global food regime and village food regime?

Research Methodology
The research on which this chapter is based is part of a larger multi-disciplinary research project entitled "Palimpsest of Agrarian Change," which has been reported elsewhere (El Nour et al. 2015; Gharios et al. 2016). This larger project is based on research conducted in South Lebanon from 2013 to 2015, addressing landscape and food-production transformations in South Lebanon from the end of the eighteenth century to the present.

This chapter is based on ethnographic fieldwork in one village, Sinay. The fieldwork was conducted from July 2013 to July 2015. The researcher spent almost two years in the village and a few weeks in Beirut. The fieldwork methods included participant observation, semi-structured interviews, life stories of practices and work trajectories of elder men in the village, and exercises and group discussions focused on wild plants and traditional foods. Many informal meetings were organized with villagers, and often discussions took place in informal settings. We interviewed about 70 people in the village, and conducted 15 live stories. The interviewees range in age between 30 and 80, and include both women and men. The semi-structured interview topics included agricultural techniques, mechanization, wage labor, the land-tenure system, flow of capital, food habits, local wild plants, and other subjects.

Interviews varied between 30 and 90 minutes in length, and took place in various locations (in the agricultural fields, in the houses of interviewees, and in my house in the village). Many of the thematic interviews were recorded, so that the discussions could be transcribed afterward. My presence in the village allowed me to collect personal documents, and stories of everyday life and practices of farmers. I made daily observation notes of my interactions with the villagers.

Study Area

Jabal 'Amil is the historical and also the local popular name of South Lebanon. The region extends over an area of around 2,000 square kilometers from the al-Awwali River to northern Palestine.

Sinay is located near the town of Ansar, in the district of al-Nabatiyya, South Lebanon, 89 kilometers from Beirut and 13 kilometers from the city of al-Nabatiyya (fig. 1).

Sinay has four hills. The villagers originally settled on one of these hills (al-Day'aa), surrounded by terraced agriculture and three other predominantly agricultural hills (Dahr al-Zayf, Karady, and Dahr al-Duhur). The valleys between these hills—*al-widyan*—shape the agricultural areas of the village. The plateau that extends from the village to

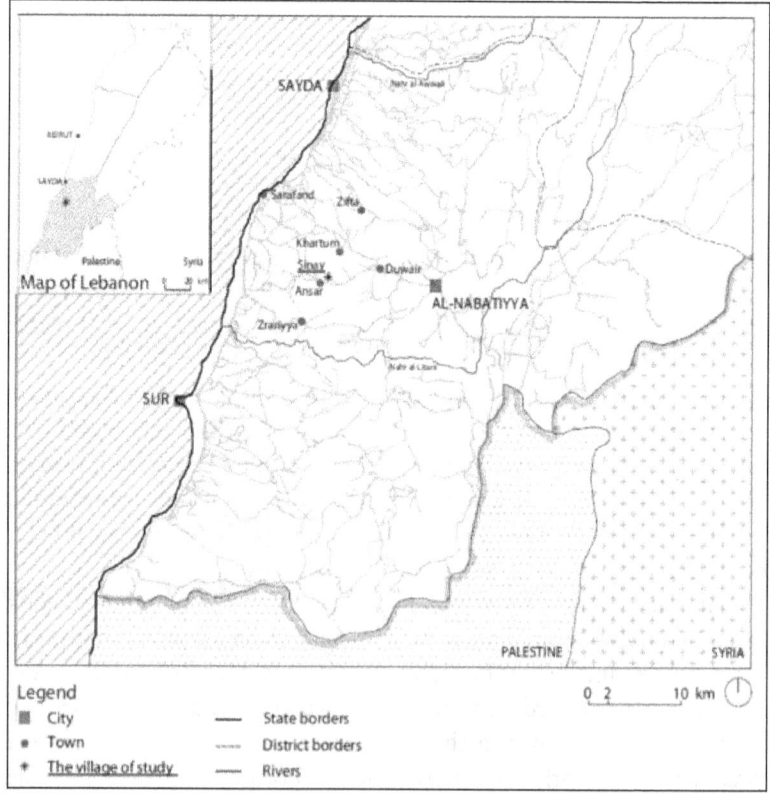

Figure 1. South Lebanon (Source: Gharios et al., 2016)

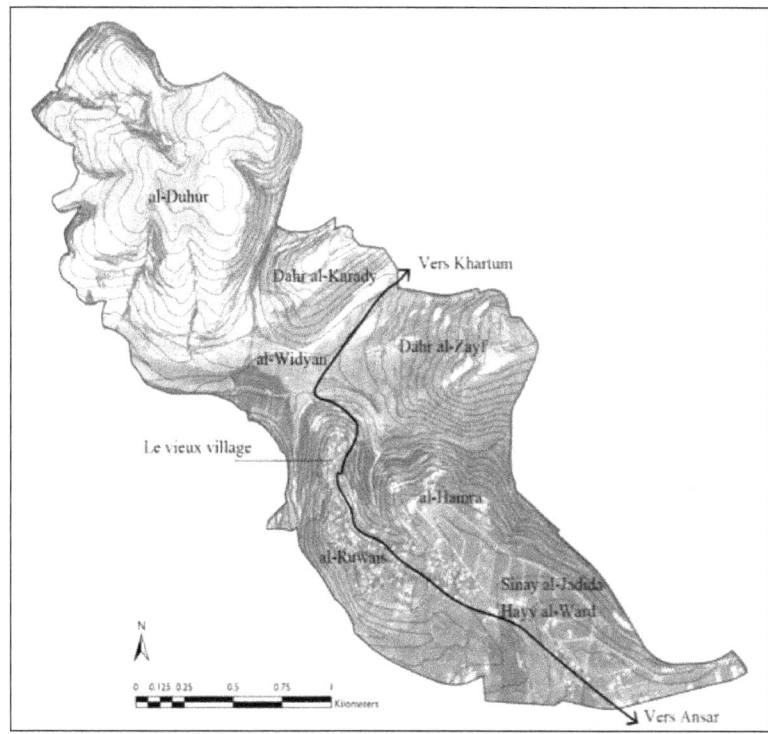

Figure 2. Sinay village (Source: Gharios *et al.*, 2016)

the southeast—known as the al-Hamra and al-Ruwais—has varied use of its land. Figure 2 is an aerial photograph of the village in 2005 to show the various zones. Topographical lines are also represented.

Results: Historical Transformations of Village Food Systems in Sinay

At the beginning of the twentieth century, Sinay was a *mazra'a*[1], owned by one landlord and mostly used for food production. As the global food regime took hold of the local agricultural systems, Sinay evolved from a *mazra'a* devoted to food production to a multifunction village. The local, regional, national, and international dynamics transformed the agri-food system in the village. From 1920 to 2015, the agri-food

---

1 A *mazra'a* (farm) is a large area of agricultural land populated by farm workers or *fellahin*, and only one owner owned most of the land.

system in the study village has seen significant shifts. Our analysis of the data identified four agri-food systems in the village.

First agri-food system, 1920s–1940: Traditional system. Mazra'a Sinay was fully owned by Yousef Bey[2] in the 1920s. Local people report that during the French mandate, the bey registered all the village land without identifying any of it as *mousha'* (commons or public domain). More than one person in the village stated that village shepherds who grazed in the *mousha'* paid tax (*miri*) to the Ottoman state.

The land tenure system during the early twentieth century was based on *aqsam*. *Aqsam* is a kind of sharecropping in which the owner provides the land while the peasants provide the labor and most of means of production. At the end of the season, the crop is divided, 60% going to the peasant and 40% to the owner. In addition to the fields farmed under *aqsam*, the peasants were permitted to cultivate some vegetables, figs, grapes, cactus trees, and olive trees around their homes. These plots of lands (generally less than 200 square meters were called locally *lagna*, *galala*, or *hakoura*. The productes from these small areas were to provide for domestic needs, or *mouna*. The agreement between landlord and peasants also included two forms of free labor. The first of these was that the peasants worked collectively for free on a piece of land dedicated to the production of wheat solely for the bey, without sharing. The second was that the peasants' wives were to clean the bey's house (*'amra*) once a week for free. These kinds of relations, inherited from the feudal system, continued throughout the Mandate period until the 1940s.

The agricultural work was done by wooden plows pulled by cows (*fedan*). The land was worked on a two-year rotation between cultivated and fallow (fig. 3). The farmer divided his plot of land into two parts. In the first half he would grow winter crops (wheat, barley, beans, and lentils) and summer crops (sesame and maizeleaving the other half as fallow land. In the next year, the two halves were reversed. The main planting season is winter, as this is the rainy season. In the summer, only a quarter of the land was planted by summer crops.

---

2 'Bek' or 'bey' is a Turkish title traditionally applied to the leaders of tribal groups. By the late nineteenth century, 'bey' had been reduced in the Ottoman Empire to an honorary title often referring to the local tax collectors and the feudal lord. This title was awarded by the sultan or his provincial representative.

Results: Historical Transformations of Village Food Systems in Sinay

Year Land	1ˢᵗ year		2ⁿᵈ year	
	Winter	Summer	Winter	Summer
Plot A	Cereal Beans	Sesame Maize	fallow	
Plot B	fallow		Cereal Beans	Sesame Maize

Figure 3. Planting rotation in the village

There were about 18 to 20 peasant families and three herdsmen for sheep and goats. The cultivated areas were not equal; their size depended on the family labor forces, cattle ownership, and the permission of the landlord. Some families farmed about 20 to 30 *dunum* and others only five to ten *dunum*.[3] The seasonal cultivation was described to me as follows: "In the winter they grew wheat for *mouna* and they sold the surplus. Beans, lentils, and barley were for *mouna*. In the summer they grew corn and sesame" (Bu Safi, informant, 91 years old).

The diet system during this period relied heavily on agricultural crops grown by local peasants, wild plants that grow in the uncultivated area surrounding the village, and to a lesser extent on animal products raised by people of the town, or on birds that they caught.

Some of the specific elements of this diet were as follows:
- Grains: barley bread and *borghol* (wheat) were the most important sources of grain.
- *Al-mogadarh*: a mixture of lentils, onions, and *borghol*, a basic and famous meal in the village and throughout southern Lebanon.
- Figs: used as a substitute for sweets and as a source of energy in the winter. Fig trees were planted around houses. The fruit was dried and kept to be eaten during the winter (*mouna al-shita*).
- Carob: an essential component of the diet. In the uncultivated areas there are many wild carob trees. It was dried and kept to be eaten during the winter (*mouna al-shita*).
- Wild vegetable plants: plants that grow wild at the end of winter and the beginning of spring, such as wild lettuce, mallow, fennel, chicory, hyssop, sage, asparagus, dock, eryngo, and green purslane. These plants are the basic meals for spring. Some are eaten raw or cooked, and some are dried and stored, such as thyme and sumac.

---
3 1 *dunum* = 1000 m² or 0.1 hectare.

- *Zaatat* (thyme): There were several types in the Sinay countryside. Green thyme is eaten fresh in the spring season. Thyme *mouna* is dried, and sesame and wild sumac are added, to be eaten all year.
- *Zohorat* (wildflowers): Flowers and aromatic plants were gathered in the spring, dried, and then drunk as an infusion with dried figs all year round.
- Animal protein: Farmers obtained part of their animal protein from the production of the same cows that were used in plowing, and from the owners of sheep and goats. Wild birds were seasonally hunted (October and November), and eaten especially during autumn and winter. Meat could also be purchased from the weekly market in Nabatiyya. One of my informants (85 years old) told me that his father rarely bought meat from the Nabatiyya market. He bought one *waqia* (about 250 gm) every two months for a family of seven.

This list supports the claim that the village diet depended mainly on local resources, both agricultural and natural. It is worth noting that there were very few olive trees in this historical period; we will see an increase in olive trees during subsequent periods. While the villagers' relationship with the market was limited, they were not disconnected from it. They had access to the largest local market (the Nabatiyya weekly market), buying some of its manufactured products and selling some surplus wheat and animal products.

Second agri-food food system, 1945–1975: Cheap food and a growing agriculture sector. In the late 1940s an expatriate turning from Senegal to Nabatiyya bought Sinay from the bey. The new owner started new relations with the village peasants, making *mougharasa*[4] contracts with them. After that point, olive trees, which were very

---

4 A *mougharasa* contract is a contract under which the peasant reclaims some of the owner's nonproductive land and plants trees on it. When the trees start to produce fruit, the peasant and the owner become equal owners of the land. "Mougharasa contracts are long-term contracts. They vary depending on the trees planted, the quality of soil, topography, water accessibility, and the farmer's effort to reclaim and plant the land" (Said 2003:77). Said explains that the contract period in Mount Lebanon was three to five years for blueberries, four to six years for grapes, seven to eight years for figs, and up to 10 or 12 years for olives (Said 2003:77). In our study village, the contract duration was 10 to 15 years for the cultivation of olives and figs.

Results: Historical Transformations of Village Food Systems in Sinay   73

limited in the first half of the twentieth century, began to spread in the village.

The owner also leased part of the land (100 *dunum*) to farmers from another village, Zefta, who cultivated tobacco. Both men and women from the village worked on these tobacco farms. While the processing steps, from cultivation to delivery, were characterized by division of labor by gender and age, it is important to note that the labor in tobacco cultivation was predominantly female. Women irrigated the tobacco seedlings while men put the seedling in the ground. When the leaves grew to a certain size, they were picked by girls. Children of both sexes transported the freshly cut tobacco leaves on donkeys from the field to the village square. Women threaded tobacco leaves onto strings, and then put the strings on a drying rack. After a few weeks, men pressed the leaves and stored them until they were delivered to the tobacco company.

This period witnessed multiple changes in dynamics. On the one hand, the peasants apparently owned farmland and olive trees and increased their holdings of cows. On the other hand, the young men of the village—the peasants' sons—began to move to Beirut to seek work after the end of the French Mandate and the start of an economic boom in the city. Between 1944 and 1975, the livelihoods of the people of the village were characterized remarkable complexity and diversity in the sources of their income.

In 1948, as the Zionists took hold of Palestine, hundreds of thousands of Palestinians entered Lebanon, especially South Lebanon. Palestinians became the chief manpower in agriculture. Sinay farmers took advantage of this migration to replace the sons of peasants who went to work in Beirut. In this way, regional events rearranged the division of labor in this South Lebanon village.

In addition to the above-mentioned changes in the village of the study and its neighboring villages, at the end of this period our key informants noted the increasing use of tractors[5] for agriculture. The first tractor used in the village was in the 1950s, and the first agriculture tractor actually purchased by a village farmer was in 1964.

---

5   Massoud Daher, in his book *Historic Roots of the Agricultural Question in Lebanon* (1983), states that the expansion of agricultural tractors in Lebanon started after the French Mandate. In 1948 the number of tractors was very few, about 64 (p. 122).

Before tractors, the average cultivated area per farmer in the village was about 20 *dunum*. The use of tractors raised this average to 150 *dunum*. The tractor made up for the absence of labor, but the cost of mechanization raised the production costs for the small farmers. This led to the withdrawal from agriculture of many farmers who could not afford the cost.

Mechanization came to dominate cereal cultivation, while manual workers (Palestinian and Lebanese) worked in the orchards and greenhouses that emerged in the 1960s and 1970s. The orchard boom was accompanied by the drilling of numerous water wells and the export of fruit to the Arab Gulf states. During this period, despite the spread of orchards in the area surrounding the village, our study village itself did not witness this phenomenon because of the lack of properties large enough for an orchard (at least 30–50 *dunum*).

This period was marked by the decline of the agrarian community in the village. Farming went from being the main occupation of the village to less than a third of the village population. The binary agriculture rotation did not change: the farmers continued their practice of cultivating only half of their land and letting the other half rest. Also, sharecropping continued to be the dominant land-tenure system, since the majority of the village land was still in the hands of a single owner from outside the village.

The prices of agricultural products decreased during the 1940s and 1950s as a result of the liberal policy adopted by the government after independence.[6] The new emerging liberal state refused to support farmers. These policies changed a bit under the presidency of Fouad Chehab in the 1960s. Chehab applied state-engagement developmental policies that caused an increase in the wheat cultivation area and in the amount of wheat delivered to the state.

It can thus be said that during this period (1940–1975) there was an expansion of wage labor and its contribution to rural families' incomes. There was also greater integration into the local diet system of industrial processed foods coming from Beirut and imported from

---

6   See A. Dagher, "How the Lebanon Countryside Was Emptied of Its Population," *al-Akhbar* newspaper, No. 1504, September 6, 2011, http://www.al-akhbar.com/node/20513

abroad. Sugar replaced dried figs. *Zhourat*[7] were replaced by tea and coffee. Rice took the place of local *borghol* and lentils. Canned beans replaced locally produced beans. During this period, the consumption of dairy and meat increased in the village, and the wild-plant component decreased. However, poor people and Palestinians continued to collect wild plants for consumption or sale. This period can be described as a gradual transition toward a diet with high meat and dairy components. It also saw an increase in fruit consumption as a result of the spread of orchards in the region, and of home-garden fruit trees such as loquat, grapes, and citrus.

Third agri-food system, 1975–1990: Civil war system. The outbreak of the civil war (1975) led to significant changes in the local power relations, livelihood strategies, and agricultural production relations, not only in our case-study village but also all over the country.

Although the sharecropping system continued during the civil war period, a local community uprising in our study village in 1975–1976 reduced the owner's share from 40% to 20%. This happened under the pressure of younger villagers involved in the communist and nationalist political parties and militias. Bu Sami (75 years old) recounts: "In 1976 there was no flour in the village as a result of the closure of the roads. So we decided that the village wheat production would not leave the village.... Also we considered that the village landowner exploited peasants and took 40% of the production without giving anything to the farmer. We decided to reduce the share of the owner. We conducted a meeting with the landowner, asking him to reduce his share of production from 40% to 20% and to sell us his share so the wheat would not leave the village, and he accepted." This system, in which the owner received 20% and the farmer received 80%, continued throughout the civil war and until the end of sharecropping in the village in 2014.

The onset of war in 1975 led to the suspension of tobacco production in the village for several reasons. Bu Khalil explains: "As the events[8] began in 1975 we stopped growing tobacco ... the girls could not get

---

7   *Zhourat* was the main local drink, a herbal tea combining wild medicinal, aromatic, and flowering plants.

8   Villagers refer to the civil war as 'the events' (*al-ahdath*), rather than 'war,' a term that they reserve for the July 2006 war, the 1948 war, and the 1982 invasion by Israel.

to the field at night to pick tobacco leaves, and the Régie[9] no longer received the yield or sent us the money."

Until 1975 immigration to Beirut was a central factor in the livelihoods of many of the people of Sinay. It contributed to the accumulation of funds that led to the improvement of agricultural production and the establishment of the properties of some of the peasants/workers, as noted in the previous section. The civil war forced many villagers to return to their village. The increased population overcrowded the village houses. Young people started to ask for land to build houses, independent from their families. They asked for 200 *dunum*—one *dunum* for each returning young man to construct his house. This demand created a conflict with one of the major landowners, which continued throughout the civil war and did not end until 1987. The landowner finally agreed to give 200 *dunum* to the villagers in return for a sum of money that was below the market price. This agreement was sponsored by the Amal movement (for more details see El Nour et al. 2015.)

During the period between the outbreak of the civil war in 1975 and the Israeli occupation of the village in 1982, the migration of villagers to West Africa accelerated. The first case of migration from the village to Abidjan, Ivory Coast was in 1976. Not surprisingly, this first migration from Sinay took place through a friendship with an emigrant from Zerareyh (a village near Sinay that has a long history of migration to Africa since the beginning of the nineteenth century). The first restaurant in Abidjan owned by someone from Sinay opened in 1978. Since then, migration from the village to Africa has gradually increased, based on kinship and lineage networks. In 2015 there were about 13 to 15 industrial and commercial enterprises owned by Sinay villagers in Ivory Coast, and more than 100 villagers who lived and worked in Africa.

Cultivation of vegetables with high added value, oriented to the wholesale market in Sidon and Beirut, also spread during this period. Greenhouses represented an important change in the agriculture system in Sinay. This system is based on control over all production-related conditions, such as drip irrigation, pest-resistant seeds, and chemical fertilization. This mode of production enjoyed a boom at first, but then

---

9   Régie Libanaise des Tabacs et Tombacs (Lebanese National Company for Tobacco and Tombac). 'Tombac' is a distinctive strain of tobacco.

quickly receded as a result of high production costs and difficulties in the transport of goods under the conditions of civil war and Israeli occupation. These conditions forced peasants to give up this mode of production, but its effect on production and consumption patterns during this period cannot be disregarded.

Between the outbreak of the civil war in 1975 and the Taif Agreement in 1990, the role of the agricultural economy in the livelihoods of the majority of the village population continued to decline, and the proportion of the population engaged in agriculture continued to fall. Agriculture did not disappear but was marginalized, although it continued to play a central role in the provision of basic food needs for some inhabitants.

The 1975–1990 period is regarded as an austere diet period. The villagers depended on local food and food aid from the militias, as well as remittances from workers abroad. The importance of money in providing for necessities increased. There was also a return to the *mouna* habits of stockpiling cereals and beans because of the circumstances of the war. During this period there was an increase in reliance on cereals and a significant shrinking of animal protein. One of my informants stated that the spread of weapons and the lack of food in this period increased the hunting of wild birds, which led to the disappearance of some bird species from the countryside surrounding the village.[10]

Overall, the civil war and the Israeli occupation had conflicting effects on the village population. While the war increased external migration, the Israeli occupation deepened the attachment to the village for both migrants and residents.

Fourth agri-food system, 1990–2000s: Double movement? After the Taif Agreement, the postwar regime in Lebanon restructured the Lebanese economy on the basis of neoliberal policies. Imported goods began to flow into the country, and cereal and meat imports increased. Consumption gluttony was supported by open-door policies, the new media, and migrant remittances.

---

10 Fayyad Fayyad, in his book *The Boy Who Was* (2014), explains that during the civil war the people of Ansar, a village adjacent to Sinay, cut down oak trees for heating and cooking and and for catching wild birds to eat. These processes have changed the "audiovisual" landscape of the village.

We can examine the example of goat production in our case-study village. Beginning in the early 1990s, there were gradual changes in the demand for goat. Bu Slah, the main herdsman of the village, gradually began reducing his herd of goats. He attributed this to a crisis in the livestock sector: "Ships loaded with sheep and cattle competed with local meat and reduced meat prices." He also blamed shrinking pastureland on the spread of urbanization, as well as the construction of roads for cars, not for humans and animals. He added that people now prefer beef. After Bu Slah's death in 2014, two of his three sons sold their shares in the herd and the third son kept about 70 down from the original 200. This son practiced grazing as a second job in addition to his work as a baker.

Cattle breeding shows the same pattern. The number of cattle in the village in 2015 was about 116, just over half the number reported for 1975 (200). The number of breeders dropped from 13 in the past to four today. One of them owns one cow, the second owns three cows, the third owns about 10 cows, and the fourth owns 100 cows. The farmer who owns one cow sells his milk in the village. The three other breeders use a system based on intensive feeding and send almost all of their milk to the dairy processor in Beirut.

We noted that during this period the value of land, and the villagers' relationship to it, seemed to change. For almost all of its inhabitants, the village changed from a place to live and work into a place for relaxation and vacations. If the 'productive value' of the village has dropped, its 'cultural value' for the local people has increased.

During the last ten years, and particularly since 2002, owning a house in the village has come to be considered a form of 'struggle' or 'resistance' for the former residents of Sinay who now live in Beirut (and who are locally known as 'Bayarta'). The commercial construction of residential buildings in Sinay by real-estate investors has increased in the last ten years. Ownership of one of these houses or apartments has become a cornerstone in the relationship of the Bayarta to their ancestral village. While the Bayarta seek to acquire a second house in the village to prove their attachment to it, the immigrants to Africa are building large villas with fenced gardens to prove their success.

The real-estate companies have taken advantage of this dynamic to launch a major construction project. They have devoted around

Results: Historical Transformations of Village Food Systems in Sinay

Table 1. National and local dimensions of Sinay agri-food system

Dimensions of agro-food system		First food system, 1920s–1940	Second food system, 1945–1975	Third food system, 1975–1990	Fourth food system, 1990–2000s
National level	National policies	French Mandate	Independence (1943–1958): laissez-faire policy. Shihabism (1958–1964): state development projects; withdrawal of US troops from Lebanon. Post 1964: back to reduction of state role.	Lebanese civil war. Militia power / Syria /Israel. 1982–1985: Israeli occupation of the area.	Haririm policies: rebuild Lebanese economy on neoliberal principles. Rental state: multiple forms of rent; financial, real estate, remittances, and strategic rent.
	Agrarian policies	Land registration. Tobacco expansion. Creation of agricultural credit bank.	Village infrastructure: electricity, water, roads. Green plan for reclamation of land and building of water reservoirs and terraces.	Rule of market. Free trade. Export-led policies.	Support for export of fruits and vegetables to Gulf countries.
Village level	Types of agrarian commodities	Wheat.	Tobacco.	Citrus, vegetables.	Land as a speculated commodity.
	Agriculture and animal production system in the village	Traditional agriculture and pastoral practices.	Mechanization and chemical fertilization of agriculture. Traditional pastoral practices.	Intensive agriculture. Water pumping. Intensive cattle production, along with traditional pastoral practices.	Marginal agriculture sector. Mechanization and chemical fertilization of agriculture. Intensive cattle production; decline of traditional pastoral practices.
	Nutrition habits	Post-famine diet. Cereal-based diet. Wild plants.	Increased consumption of local dairy products. Imports of cheap foods.	Minimal diet, relying on local production. Food aid from militias and international sources.	Multiple trajectories: 'Westernization' of diets. Greater reliance on markets. Source of local food regime: wild plants and the emergence of alternative local food networks.
	Labor	New feudal relations. Family labor.	Wage boom. Female wage labor. Palestinian labor.	Migrant workers: Syrian and Egyptian.	Foreign workers: Syrian women and refugees.

Dimensions of agro-food system		First food system, 1920s–1940	Second food system, 1945–1975	Third food system, 1975–1990	Fourth food system, 1990–2000s
	Environmental changes	Traditional land conservation, refertilization, crop rotation. Recycling of wastes.	Environmental problems resulting from excessive use of mechanization, fertilizer, and pesticide.	Concerns over pesticides. Remnants of war. Global climate change.	Soil and nutrition degradation. Loss of village forest (*mousha'*) land. Waste management issues: garbage disposal in wilderness areas.

(Source: Author's fieldwork analysis)

two-thirds of the previously vacant land to building 'New Sinay City.' Land speculation has caused the price of 1000 square meters of land in the village to increase from 15,000 dollars in 1990 to 150,000 in 2015.

Summary of historical changes. The agri-food system in the village witnessed significant changes during the period under study. Dependent at the beginning of the twentieth century mainly on domestic production (natural and agricultural), it became more and more dependent on the market to provide not only manufactured goods, but most agricultural products as well.

The transition in the diet system was caused by multiple factors, notably changes in the income source and employment structure of villagers, the social and class reconfiguration after the transfer of land via *mougharasa* between 1945 and 1975, and the marginalization of the agrarian community. Nevertheless, wild and agricultural domestic production did not end completely, nor has it been eliminated from the diet of the local population. I observed the return of local elements in the diet driven by social and cultural factors linked to local identity, nostalgia, and new food culture promoted by urban weekend visitors or the media, as well as by economic need in some cases.

The village diet system today is characterized by complexity and the overlap of two contradictory transitions. The first is a westernized diet system, characterized by increased consumption of meat and industrial goods after the spread of shops and as a result of massacres in and around the village. The second is a localized diet system associated with the growth of demand for local agricultural and natural products.

Discussion

To understand the relations between village agri-food dynamics and the national and global contexts, we analyzed the village agri-food system dynamic in relation to the larger structural context. Tables 1 and 2 combine three structural levels—the village agri-food system (micro structure), the national level (meso-structure), and global food regime dynamics (large structure).

At the national level, the dynamics of the capitalist system cannot in themselves explain what happened in Lebanon. Michael Gilsenan (1996), in his seminal study about Akkar in the early twentieth century, explained the role of the French Mandate in the extension of the feudal system and the support of some regional leaders in the marginalized areas. We observed the same process in southern Lebanon: the role of the French Mandate in the consolidation of the feudal system in the village of study until the late 1930s.

Baalbaki (1985) explains that the integration of Lebanon into the global market is not new; it has existed since the seventeenth century. He makes a distinction between the capitalist transformation and integration into the market. The grain trade is old, for example, but the mode of production did not become capitalist until the mid twentieth century. The open-market policies adopted by Lebanon directly after independence led to the destruction of grain and livestock production and some fruits, while horticulture and the poultry and industrial sectors benefited (Baalbaki 1985; Tarabulsi 2014). Between 1945 and 1970 the cultivation of citrus expanded, benefiting from cheap, skilled Palestinian labor and from demand in the Arabian Gulf markets. The 1960s saw the development of packaging, refrigeration, and marketing by agricultural production companies (Baalbaki 1985).

For Tarabulsi (2014), the reason for the deterioration of Lebanese agricultural production is that the national economy is now based on the trade and services sectors (especially financial services). This qualifies Lebanon as a 'rentier state'—that is, a state that depends on external sources of funding. In our case, this funding takes various forms: financial services, real estate, migrant remittances, and international aid.

Agricultural transformations were not a prelude to the capitalist transformation and were not linked to industrialization, which was deliberately neglected (either by the Mandate authority or by the

Table 2. Characteristics of global food regimes based on the theoretical framework of Friedmann and McMichael (1989)

Dimensions of theory	First food regime (1870–1914)	Second food regime (1940s–1970s)	Third food regime (1980s–2000s)
Major international power	Britain as the center, with settlers and occupied colonies.	US as the center, with US food aid to help 'national development.' Third-world countries as informal colonies. Emergence of TNCs.	Multiple centers (US, UK, Japan) and TNCs. Emergence of alternative food networks. Multiple trajectories.
International policies	Developing national agricultural model. International trade based on imperial influence.	Protectionism. Government-supported agriculture.	Market rule. Free trade. GATT-based policies, cutting subsidies and tariffs. Patent-based practices.
Type of commodities	Wheat, meat, tropical/colonial products.	Cheap foods and livestock. US 'meat/soy/maize complex.'	Northern grain exports to South. Southern export of 'exotics' to North.
Dominant forms of capital	British (and other European) industrial capital.	Growing power, and transnationalization, of agribusiness capital.	Corporate agribusiness capital.
Nutrition relations	Energy and protein for low-wage workers and industrial classes.	Diet-related diseases (starvation and obesity).	'Westernization' of diets.
Agricultural practice	Exploitative use of land. Extension of cultivated area.	Intensive agriculture. Agro-industrialization (mechanization and 'chemicalization' of agriculture).	Biotechnology-based intensive agriculture: GMOs, biopiracy. Mounting ecological devastation.
Environmental change	Soil and nutrition degradation. Loss of forests.	Environmental problems resulting from excessive use of mechanization, fertilizers, and pesticides.	Concerns over pesticides. Food safety and GMOs. Global climate change.
'Alternatives'	Tensions/contradictions in occupied area and in colonial centers.	Localization of food production and distribution. Democratic food policy.	La Via Campesina. Food sovereignty. Localized production, distribution, and consumption.

(Sources: Friedmann and McMichael 1989; Le Heron 1993; McMichael 2009; Dixon 2009; Campbell 2009)

Conclusion

independence governments). The dismantling of feudal modes of production was not the result of shifts in production capacity, but of shifts in consumption and lifestyle changes for the upper class. Rents from agricultural production were not able to satisfy the lifestyle and consumer demands of the landholding families, so they sold the land. This solution enabled the emergence of small and medium properties, mostly concerned with the achievement of small-scale capitalist agriculture. Secondary capitalist agriculture led by expatriates, traders, and professionals has also grown (Baalbaki 1985).

While the global food system is divided into three phases (see table 2), our analysis of the local food regimes in Lebanon is based on the distinction between four stages (see table 1). By comparing tables 1 and 2, we can see that the relationship between transformations at the village level and the global level is not automatic. The effects of the global system may or may not appear directly in the diet trends if local public policies and regional conflict have had a greater influence on the agri-food system in the village. For example, the delayed appearance of capitalist agriculture is linked to the nature of the relationship between local elites and the colonial powers. The mechanization of agriculture is linked to the international migration of the local young men. Delay in switching to a western diet is caused by regional conflicts.

The transformations of the agri-food system in the study village is characterized by complexity and an overlap between local, regional, and global influences. It has followed a non-linear trajectory, combining the different variables according to local and regional conditions.

Conclusion

The case study of Sinay provides a deep understanding of the transformations of the agricultural and food habits in rural Lebanon. It shows the influence of cultural and social elements on the pattern of food habits and the resilience of the relationship between society and nature. We can summarize the driving factors for the change as urbanization, food-habit dynamics, import and external market growth, the shrinking of the agrarian community and the relative importance of agriculture, war and liberation of the village, and finally the reevaluation of local food culture.

Although many studies indicate that the dietary pattern in Lebanon is the most westernized in the Arab world, our field evidence confirms the existence of an overlap between the traditional diet, based on local wild and cultivated plants, and the western diet based on animal protein.

With regard to the village food-system dynamic in South Lebanon, the key contribution of this chapter is to call attention to the local dynamics implicit in national and international agri-food relations. The analysis shows the uneven transformation of the agri-food system of the village to totally westernized and globalized structures. Western food cultures, institutions, and technologies (such as supermarkets, fast-food chains, microwaves, and refrigerators) are becoming increasingly important in local food systems. However, the village diet continues to combine imported products and traditional foods. Indeed, the transition does not systematically lead to a decline in traditional foods, but instead leads to the emergence of hybrid diets.

The agri-food dynamics in Sinay can be viewed as a double movement—the clash of two opposed and incompatible principles. On the one hand is the principle of the market economy; on the other hand is the desire of a society to impose its own values on the process of the production and distribution of food. In other words, the dynamics of the village agri-food system are shaped by the articulations between the embedded economy and its opposite—the disembedded economy.[11]

References

Baalbaki, A. 1985. *Lebanese Agriculture and State Interventions in the Countryside between Independence and Civil War*. Beirut and Paris: Owaidat.

Bernstein, H. 2015. *Food Regimes and Food Regime Analysis: A Selective Survey*. Chiang Mai Conference Paper Series 1. Accessed January 2016 at http://www.iss.nl/fileadmin/ASSETS/iss/Research_and_projects/Research_networks/LDPI/CMCP_1-_Bernstein.pdf

---

11 I would like to thank the Palimpsest of Agrarian Change project, on which I worked as Postdoctoral Researcher. This project was funded by the Emirates Foundation for Philanthropy as part of the LSE Academic Collaboration with Arab Universities Programme. It was administered by the LSE Middle East Centre and by the Faculty of Agricultural and Food Sciences of the American University of Beirut, under the aegis of Professors Rami Zurayk and Martha Mundy, Senior Researchers. I would also like to thank Cynthia Gharios, Junior Researcher, for her exceptional help and collaboration.

References

Campbell, H. 2009. "Breaking New Ground in Food Regime Theory: Corporate Environmentalism, Ecological Feedbacks and the 'Food from Somewhere' Regime?" *Agriculture and Human Values*, 26(4): 309.

Chinnakonda, D., & Telford, L. 2007. *Local and Regional Food Economies in Canada: Status Report*. Ottawa: Agriculture and Agri-Food Canada.

Hinrichs, C. C. 2000. "Embeddedness and Local Food Systems: Notes on Two Types of Direct Agricultural Market," *Journal of Rural Studies*, 16(3): 295–303.

Daher, M. 1983. *Historical Roots of the Agricultural Question in Lebanon, 1900-1950*. Beirut: Lebanese University Press.

Dixon, J. 2009. "From the Imperial to the Empty Calorie: How Nutrition Relations Underpin Food Regime Transitions," *Agriculture and Human Values*, 26: 321–333.

Fayyad, F. 2014. *The Boy Who Was: Memories and Thoughts*. Beirut: Dar Mawasem.

Friedma, H., & McMichael, P. 1989. "Agriculture and the State System: The Rise and Decline of National Agricultures, 1870 to the Present," *Sociologia Ruralis*, 29(2): 93–117.

Gharios, C., S. El Nour, M. Mundy, and R. Zurayk. 2016. "Transformation Rurale, Paysage et Conflit dans un Village du Liban Sud, Sinay," *Economie Rurale*, March–April: 353–354.

Gilsenan, M. 1996. *Lords of the Lebanese Marches: Violence and Narrative in an Arab Society*. Oakland: University of California Press.

Goodman, D. 1997. "World-scale Processes and Agro-food Systems: Critique and Research Needs," *Review of International Political Economy*, 4(4): 663–687.

Haapanen, T. 2011. *Rural Food System Change in Tanzania During the Post-Ujamaa Era: A Case Study from Western Bagamoyo District*. Turku (Finland): Turun Yliopisto.

Jablonski, R., and M. Yuri. 2012. "Local Food Wholesale Infrastructure in New York State: Economic Impact, Policy Implications and Recommendations." AAEA/EAAE Food Environment Symposium, May 30–31, 2012, Boston, MA.

Kaufman, J., and P. Kameshwari. 2000. "The Food System: A Stranger to the Planning Field," *Journal of the American Planning Association*, 66(2): 113–124.

Le Heron, R. and N.Lewis, 2009. "Discussion. Theorising Food Regimes: Intervention as Politics," *Agriculture and Human Values*, 26:345–349.

Le Mouël, C., A. Forslund, P. Marty, S. Manceron, E. Marajo-Petitzon, M.-A. Caillaud, and B. Schmitt. 2015. *Le système agricole et alimentaire de la région Afrique du Nord–Moyen-Orient à l'horizon 2050: Projections de tendance et analyse de sensibilité. Rapport final de l'étude réalisée pour le compte de Pluriagri*. Paris and Rennes: INRA-DEPE & INRA-SAE2.

Love, J. B. 2010. *Hezbollah: Social Services as a Source of Power*. JSOU Report 10-5. Hurlburt Field, FL: Joint Special Operations University. Accessed January 2016 at https://www.wikileaks.org/gifiles/attach/14/14771_JSOU10-5loveHezbollah_final-1.pdf

Machado, N. 2011. "Karl Polanyi and the New Economic Sociology: Notes on the Concept of (Dis)embeddedness," *RCCS Annual Review*, October 1. Accessed March 28, 2016. http://rccsar.revues.org/309; DOI: 10.4000/rccsar.309

Martinez, S., M. Hand, M. Pra, et al. 2013. *Local Food Systems: Concepts, Impacts, and Issues*. Report 97. Washington, DC: United States Department of Agriculture Economic Research.

McMichael, P., 2004. "Global Development and the Corporate Food Regime." Symposium on New Directions in the Sociology of Global Development, XI World Congress of Rural Sociology, Trondheim. July. http://www.iatp.org/files/451_2_37834.pdf. Accessed January 2017.

———. 2009. "A Food Regime Genealogy," *Journal of Peasant Studies*, 36(1): 139–170.

Ministry of Agriculture. 2014. *Ministry of Agriculture Strategy 2015–2019*. Beirut: Ministry of Agriculture.

El Nour, S., C. Gharios, M. Mundy, and R. Zurayk. 2015. "The Right to the Village? Concept and History in a Village of South Lebanon," *Justice spatiale/Spatial Justice*, 7. Online at www.jssj.org/wp-content/uploads/2015/01/El-Nour-Liban-EN-avec-illust.pdf

Polanyi, K. 1957. *The Great Transformation: The Political and Economic Origins of Our Time*. Boston: Beacon Press.

Read, R. S. D., and G. P. Jones. 2002. "The Food Supply." In M. L. Wahlqvist, ed., *Food and Nutrition: Australasia, Asia and the Pacific*, 37–48. Crows Nest (Australia): Allen & Unwin.

References

Said, A. 2003. *Social and Economic Relations in the Lebanese Countryside, 1861–1914*. Beirut : Dar Al-Farabi.

Thompson, E., Jr., A. M. Harper, and S. Kraus. 2008. "Think Globally—Eat Locally: San Francisco Foodshed Assessment, American Farmland Trust." https://www.google.fr/url?sa=t&rct=j&q=&esrc=s&source=web&cd=&ved=0ahUKEwiQkIaOytjRAhWBVhQKHZTxDQAQFggcMAA&url=http%3A%2F%2Fwww.thegreenhorns.net%2Fwp-content%2Ffiles_mf%2F1340378421SanFranciscoFoodShedAssessment.pdf&usg=AFQjCNHbWQwaA7uXpeq9J7xkfs3i3vvImw&sig2=d8XOBOQJ77qY2DGx5uaOtg&cad=rja. Accessed January 2016.

Tarabulsi, F. 2014. *Social Classes and Political Power in Lebanon*. Beirut: Heinrich Böll Stiftung.

United Nations Environment Programme. 2005. *Effects of Trade Liberalization on Agriculture in Lebanon: With Special Focus on Products Where Methyl Bromide Is Used*. Geneva: UNEP.

CHAPTER 6

Food Issues and Revolution: The Process of Dispossession, Class Solidarity, and Popular Uprising: The Case of Sidi Bouzid in Tunisia

Habib Ayeb

> "Being a Marxist doesn't excuse you from taking a close look."
>
> Maurice Godelier

After more than three decades of forced absence from research agendas and budgets, the world food crisis of 2007 and 2008 restored food and agriculture to an important place in academic work and research, as well as in the reflections and actions of civil-society organizations, especially peasant organizations and associations. Furthermore, the world food crisis set off by the brutal rise in the prices of basic foodstuffs, such as cereals,[1] had the fortunate effect of revealing to decision-makers and political activists, as well as to the wider public, the extent of the structural dependence of local (village-level) agriculture on the 'global food and agricultural market.' Within just a few months, almost the whole world suddenly became aware that the rhythm of good and bad harvests (that is, good and bad farm years) was no longer tied solely to the local climate or local conditions, but also, and especially, to the evolution of the international market in raw materials and agricultural products. States that were accustomed

---

1 Overall, world food prices in 2008 were 83% higher than in 2005. The price of wheat rose by 130% and the price of rice doubled in the first three months of 2008. The FAO food price index increased by more than 40% in 2008, compared with 9% in 2007.

to meeting their food needs by imports quickly realized that, after a certain threshold price, their access to world markets had become limited, if not impossible. This was notably the case for Tunisia, which had built its entire farm and food policy on the principle of "comparative advantage"[2] and of food security. It prioritized the export of out-of-season agricultural products (early crops, such as fruit, certain vegetables, flowers, etc.) and of olive oil (of which Tunisia was the leading exporter worldwide in 2015), and the import of basic products including cereals and vegetable oils.[3]

Still, in spite of the rarity of academic studies on food issues before the world food crisis, current research cannot ignore the foundational studies that, beginning in the early 1980s, launched the analyses and debates on the issue. We may cite as examples the works of Friedmann and McMichael that introduced the concepts of 'food system' and 'food regime' (Friedman 1982; 1987; 1993; 1994; Friedmann and McMichael 1989). Moreover, in the realm of civil society and civil associations, we may mention the initiative of the international peasant organization Via Campesina, which introduced the concept of 'food sovereignty.' This organization actively works to mobilize peasants and their associations and unions worldwide (notably but not exclusively in the global South), so as to take an active part in this new alternative.

Nonetheless, reflection and debate on the connections between 'food politics' and popular 'uprisings' and 'revolts' remain relatively rare, even though recent decades have seen several revolts, especially in the South, directly provoked by political initiatives such as raising the prices of basic foodstuffs or of agricultural inputs. In Tunisia, there were bread riots in 1984, which followed almost immediately upon an unexpected rise in the

---

2 "The principle of comparative advantage, also called the principle of comparative costs, can be stated as follows: Under the necessary and sufficient condition that there exists a difference between the comparative costs of self-sufficiency in several countries, each of them will find it to their advantage to specialize, exporting the goods in which it enjoys the greatest comparative advantage (or the least comparative disadvantage), and importing other goods from its partners in exchange." Lassudrie-Duchêne and Ünal-Kesenci 2001:1.

3 Tunisia imports 75% of its hard wheat (couscous, breads, pasta, etc.), 20% of its soft wheat (pastries, pasta, etc.), and close to 100% of its vegetable oils, but exports the majority of its olive oil.

price of bread.[4] On a broader scale, numerous revolts followed agricultural reforms that the peasants perceived as a political desire to reduce their access to land and other agricultural resources, with the aim of excluding them completely from the agricultural sector, to the profit of agribusiness. This was notably the case in 1997 in Egypt, following the introduction of liberal agrarian reforms (Law 96 of 1992), adopted in 1992 and put into effect on October 1, 1997 (Ayeb and Bush 2014; Ayeb 2010; Saad 2002).

The revolution in Tunisia—particularly in its accelerated phase from December 17, 2010 (the self-immolation of Muhammad Bouazizi) to January 14, 2011 (the flight of the dictator Ben Ali)—was largely fed by the prevailing feeling among the peasants that the agricultural policies being followed by the government aimed at marginalizing them and depriving them of agricultural and food resources.

By reviewing the unfolding of the revolutionary process in Tunisia, in both its long phase (2008–2011) and its accelerated phase (December 2010–January 2011), this chapter seeks to demonstrate the direct connection between the process of dispossession and impoverishment of the Sidi Bouzid peasantry (by, and to the advantage of, agribusiness) and the demonstrations of solidarity with Bouazizi against the state, which the peasants viewed as directly responsible for their collective troubles and for the death of one of their own. The chapter will try to show that what was at work was, to a certain extent, a 'class solidarity' of the rural and peasant community directed toward another peasant—or, at least, someone who was considered as such—and against the class (social group) of big-city investors and representatives of the state.

Sidi Bouzid after the Suicide of Muhammad Bouazizi: A Local Segment of a Global Revolutionary Process

There are dates and names that engrave themselves permanently in a community's collective memory, and sometimes go beyond it to occupy a significant place in the collective history. This is true of December

---

4 "During this period, social conflict took on an essentially urban character, thanks to the union struggles led by the Union Générale Tunisienne du Travail (UGTT). These led to the events of January 1978 (general strike and demonstrations in the major cities, such as Tunis and Sfax), and the bread revolt in January 1984 (popular strikes in the major cities in protest against increases in the prices of foodstuffs, especially bread). These strikes were put down at the cost of blood. The political opposition, particularly the left, was muzzled, and freedom of the press was severely curtailed" (Daoud 2001:4).

17, 2010, of Sidi Bouzid, and, of course, of Muhammad Bouazizi. An ordinary date, like all the 365 days of the year, and two unknown, even anonymous names—a city and a person—that no one suspected would occupy such a significant place in either geography or history. Nevertheless, all three are known almost everywhere in the world, and they will long remain in our individual and collective memories. But why this date and these names particularly? After all, probably not a day goes by when someone, in Tunisia or elsewhere, doesn't end his own life. So why has this particular suicide impressed itself as a key moment in the contemporary history not just of Tunisia, but of the entire region and probably well beyond it?

The reasons are many, in all likelihood. But one of them stands out: Sidi Bouzid is not so ordinary a region as one might think, and Muhammad Bouazizi is far from being a simple, anonymous person, even if no one outside his own circle of family and friends knew him. For the past 30 years, Sidi Bouzid has been a region suffering rapid and violent economic, ecological, political, social, and even landscape change, induced by a state policy that seeks to make of this arid region of central Tunisia a center for intensive and 'modern' agricultural production, oriented toward the national market and export.

This statement is obviously surprising, especially if one is unaware of the deep disruptions that the populations of the region have seen. It is even more normal that the greatly mediatized presentation of Muhammad Bouazizi and his suicide made no connection with the agricultural policies and the situation of the peasants in Sidi Bouzid, preferring the made-up story of a young, unemployed university graduate who felt humiliated by the slap he received from a policewoman. In reality, far from being the target of this unfortunate policewoman,[5] Muhammad Bouazizi is just one of the very numerous direct victims of an aggressive, liberal model of agricultural development imposed on the region by the state, beginning at the end of the 1980s. His life history, and especially his dramatic end, are similar, if not identical, to those of hundreds and possibly thousands of small peasants subjected to fierce competition for agricultural resources (including land and irrigation water), which places them in violent opposition to

---

5 Invented from whole cloth, the story of the slap earned the policewoman more than four months in prison without trial, before she was cleared of all suspicion and acknowledged by the court as totally innocent.

the powerful investors and speculators who see nothing in this region but an unexpected opportunity to accumulate more profits and wealth, with the consent, even the encouragement, of the national and regional public authorities. These peasants are forced into a difficult choice. They can try to resist and stay where they are, at the risk of finding themselves progressively marginalized and isolated. They can "sell" their land to investors, under the influence of direct or indirect pressure (friendly or otherwise), of their urgent need for money, of the attractiveness of a large sum, of the impossibility of continuing their agricultural activity for lack of means, and so on, at the risk of becoming landless peasants and cheap labor for the new owners. Or they can move somewhere else: to the nearest town, to other cities, or abroad, in search of new sources of income.

For those who choose to remain on their land, a highly speculative and risky solution is available: they can "take advantage of" credits, usually through the banking system, to try to convert to irrigated farming, and thus bring themselves into line with the new agricultural policies. Even if the rare individual succeeds at this, more or less, the majority meet with failure, made worse by the frequent complication of forcibly losing their land, the conservation of which was precisely why they tried to convert in the first place. The credit trap that the Banque Nationale Agricole (BNA) does not hesitate to offer to reluctant smallholders consists of encouraging them to sign a credit contract for investment or equipment, mortgaging their land as collateral.[6] But since these conversions cannot be carried out without resources, most of these new small "investors" fail, and thus find themselves insolvent and unable to pay back the money they have borrowed. Consequently, the BNA sells off the mortgaged and seized land at public auction, to the highest bidder, in order to recuperate the unpaid loan. Since this scenario has repeated itself a bit too frequently for nearly three decades now, one is justified in wondering whether each one of these is a case of "organized bankruptcies," with a view to facilitating access to land and other agricultural resources for "foreign" investors,[7]

---

6 These are credits granted relatively easily to "fragile" or "insolvent" borrowers, with the intention of legally dispossessing them, in the short term, of part or all of their property—more specifically, of their real estate. This is strongly reminiscent of the "subprime crisis" in the United States, which gave rise to the great worldwide financial crisis between 2007 and 2011.

7 'Foreigners,' or less often 'settlers,' are the two rather pejorative terms by which the local peasants designate investors from other regions of the country.

often customers of the same bank. This process lends a sort of juridical legality to these operations of organized dispossession against smallholders by—and to the benefit of—the investors, the majority of whom are not natives of the region.[8]

Before proceeding further, let us pause for a moment to describe the life of the person who set himself on fire on December 17. This will provide some very useful information on the various processes that preceded, accompanied, and followed this desperate act, of which they are the cause and/or the consequence.

Muhammad Bouazizi was neither a university graduate nor a rebel. In reality, he was only one of the numerous direct victims of the processes of monopolizing land and local resources encouraged by the state on the pretext of strengthening the 'food security' that the development of export agriculture was supposed to guarantee. His father, a former farm worker, had died, leaving three young children including Muhammad, who was only three at the time. The family inherited a parcel of steppe land of less than three hectares, not irrigated and grossly inadequate to support a whole family. Some time later, the widowed mother married her brother-in-law (brother of her husband and uncle of her children).[9]

In order to increase their income, the newly formed family tried to launch a small agricultural project on their parcel by converting it to irrigation, thanks to an offer of credit from the BNA in exchange for a mortgage on the land. Unfortunately, luck was not on their side, and the family found itself heavily in debt to the bank, without the slightest hope of being able to repay. The mechanical chain was set in motion: seizure and resale of the land by the bank, loss of the family's sole source of income, and loss as well of material and symbolic capital, which plunged the family into disorder.

---

8 In such cases, the public auctions are often organized in a very obscure way, with no real communication or announcement, so as to favor potential customers who have been individually informed that the property will be up for sale. Several sources have confirmed that there was only one potential purchaser at an auction, who thus acquired the land at a low price, with no challenge from other potential buyers. The BNA is far from innocent or above suspicion in these cases of corruption.

9 This practice still exists in certain rural, conservative regions and families. The justification is that the uncle is best situated to care for his nephews and nieces and to protect their mother.

At the beginning of the 2000s, Muhammad was a farm worker with another peasant uncle, who had the same unfortunate agricultural experience: credit, missed deadlines, seizure and loss of the mortgaged land. Muhammad, once again out of work, decided to become an informal vegetable seller, and equipped himself with a cart and other items necessary to the work of a tradesman, such as scales and other small tools. However, he failed to take into account the harassment from the administrative authorities and the police officers, who did everything they could to prevent him from working normally. They kept stepping up their harassment and pressure of various kinds, until that fateful December 17 when they seized his work equipment (i.e., his scales and cart). Furious, frustrated, and desperate, he ended up committing the last act of resistance of which he felt capable.[10] With his gesture of hopelessness and revolt, Muhammad Bouazizi, without intending to, gave an accelerating push and opened the "accelerated sequence" of the global revolutionary process that was already largely under way, even if no one, including researchers and other observers, was quite conscious of it. The result is well known.

It should be emphasized here that the sequence of events, as well as Bouazizi's own trajectory, show that, in a certain sense, he did not "commit suicide" but "was suicided"—explaining why, unlike other cases, his death provoked the extraordinary spontaneous solidarity that ensued.

"Individual" Suicide and Class Solidarity

To fully understand the reasons for, and the extent of, the unexpected acceleration of the political upheavals that it provoked, Muhammad Bouazizi's desperate act must be grasped by setting it, on the one hand, in the familial and personal context that we have just seen, and, on the other hand, in a wider context[11] of local rejection of the agricultural policies imposed by the state in the name of development

---

10 For more details, see the article by Mathilde Fautras in *Jadaliyya*: http://www.jadaliyya.com/pages/index/18630/mohamed-bouazizi-louvrier-agricole_-relire-la

11 "In order to understand the behavior of individuals, one must understand the mental universe in which these individuals evolve. There are . . . two possible explanations for each behavior or each situation. One explanation associates them with the mode of production and with the economic base, while the other is based on the conceptions and definitions of the situation that are shared among the persons concerned. The first functions at the level of society, the second at the level of the individual as a member of that society" (Hopkins 1983:10–11).

and of the modernization of the country and its economy. This (re) placing into context is indispensable in order to understand why, unlike other cases, Bouazizi's suicide was "spontaneously" followed by immense "popular" demonstrations that ended in the rapid fall (less than a month!) of the Ben Ali dictatorship, which had been thought to be too solid to break. Was this a spontaneous movement on the family or tribal level, as some have claimed? Was it a "manipulation" organized by the unions (in the UGTT [Union Générale Tunisienne du Travail] case) or by political groups and parties in order to mobilize "the people" against the regime, as others have said and written? Or is it instead a question of "class solidarity," which recognizes in Bouazizi a victim of the opposition between the ruling classes ('foreigners') and the ruled classes (local communities)?

Without a long revolutionary process[12] and a certain 'class consciousness,'[13] the death of Muhammad Bouazizi would probably never have gone past the stage of "miscellaneous news" and December 17 would have remained an unimportant date, just like December 16. Thus it is important to re-situate the "accelerated sequence" (December 17, 2010–January 14, 2011) within the framework of the global revolutionary process that had begun well before December 2010 and that continues to the present time. Basing our analysis on the continuity of challenges and collective resistance (demonstrations, strikes, sit-ins), which implies a "process," it seems pertinent to situate the beginning of the global revolutionary process in the month of January 2008, with the massive strikes of the phosphate-mine workers in the southwest (beginning in Redayef), which lasted until June of the same year in spite

---

12 A revolutionary process presupposes a series of anti-establishment events relatively close together and connected to each other, while a revolt can come about within a time frame that is well defined and delimited in time and space, with no direct connection to previous events. A revolution fits within a longer period of time; it can take place in several different places and undergo a sort of continuous propagation.

13 N. S. Hopkins writes in his book about Testour: "In order for a class to exist as a social group in conflict with the class that is dialectically opposite to it, it must be formed of an aggregate of individuals whose lived experience has been formed, first, by working conditions, and then by struggle; in sum, individuals whose common perception of their material interests has been forged through easy and frequent contact and a consciousness that presupposes a terminology or a vocabulary to express its symbols. In other words, each class needs to have a structure and a discourse, a means of representing its consciousness, that can articulate the conflict" (Hopkins 1983:53).

"Individual" Suicide and Class Solidarity

of the fierce repression exercised by the state[14] against the strikers and their families. These were followed by numerous other similar actions throughout the south, the east, and the center of the country up until December 17, 2010 (Ayeb 2011; 2012).

Nevertheless, it would seem that, even if Muhammad Bouazizi's gesture fits well into this long process, the local solidarity expressed by the first demonstrations that followed it can be explained only by the local context of the events of collective resistance that took place in the region, and in relation to the profound upheavals brought on by the creation of agricultural development as a focus of activity, which has already been mentioned and which will be developed below, and by its dramatic social, economic, and ecological consequences. These have led to a broad feeling of injustice among the local population, who hold the state directly responsible for them.[15]

Among the numerous events preceding December 17, 2010, we must recall the demonstrations organized by the peasants in June and July 2010 in downtown Sidi Bouzid, in front of the provincial government building. The origin of their discontent was claims in connection with drinking water and irrigation water, farmland, subsidies, and agricultural inputs, whose prices had risen considerably, not to mention the behavior of the 'foreign' investors, who were seen as aggressive and

---

14 In December 2008, 38 union workers were brought to trial. Five were released, but the others were condemned to punishments ranging from suspended prison sentences of two years to ten years' actual imprisonment. The six leaders of the movement received the maximum sentence, accused of having "taken the lead in demonstrations that damaged public order, during which rocks and Molotov cocktails were thrown at the police," in a trial denounced by their defenders as "a parody of justice." Strong international reaction led to the review of the convictions on appeal. But in February 2009, the Gafsa appeals court changed only slightly the first verdict against the thirty or so defendants and handed down very harsh sentences. Thus Adnane Hajji (now a deputy), the mouthpiece of the movement, and Bechir Laabidi saw their sentences increased to eight years' imprisonment. Nevertheless, the defendants took advantage of this trial to show the extent of torture, systematic ill-treatment, and corruption.

15 "Without the help and support of the state, before and after 2011, which does nothing to restrain them, these despised and greedy settlers wouldn't last 24 hours here." This statement is drawn from an interview conducted in March 2016 with a landless peasant living near the town of Sidi Bouzid. In my opinion, it reveals an unquestionable and fairly elevated political consciousness.

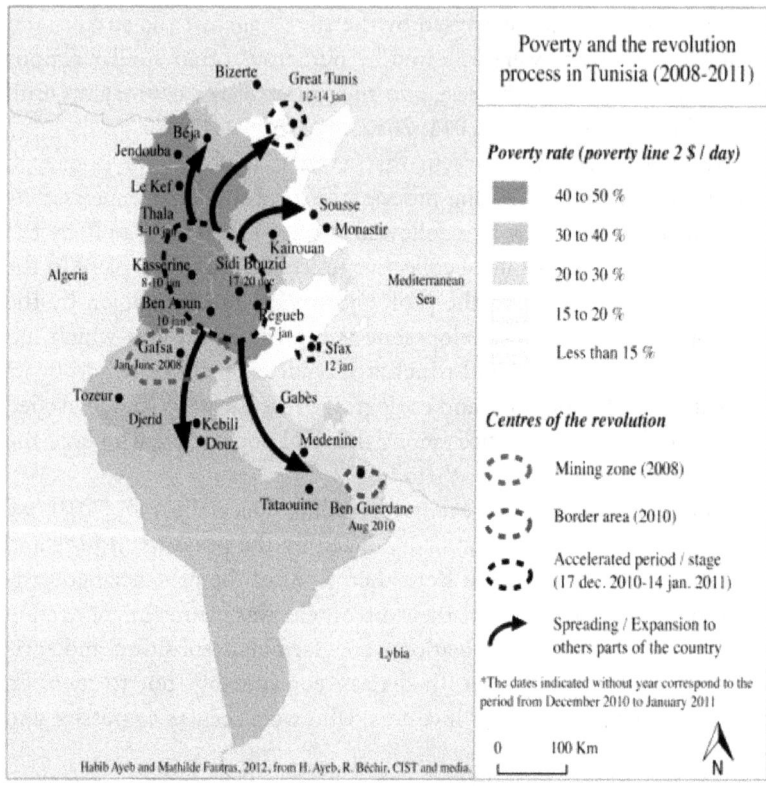

Fig. 1. Poverty and the revolution process in Tunisia, 2008–2011 (Ayeb and Faudras 2012)

disdainful.[16] But there was also the huge problem of peasant debt, in the form of credits with the BNA or of unpaid bills with the STEG (Société tunisienne de l'électricité et du gaz), mostly for the electricity

---

16 During discussions and interviews with peasants from the Sidi Bouzid region, they often accused the investors, the majority of whom came from the cities of Sfax or Tunis and other coastal cities, of being disdainful and aggressive. Many times I heard them call the investors "racist." One reason that could explain this resentment, beyond the competition over land and water, is the fact that some of the investors prefer to bring in workers from their own regions (especially from Sfax and Sousse) for the labor-intensive seasons, such as the olive, fruit, and vegetable harvests. Their pretext is that the people of Sidi Bouzid are lazy, do not know how to work properly, and cannot be trusted. In any case, mistrust between the two groups is more or less the rule.

used for pumping irrigation water. In fact, the accumulated debt of the peasants, especially the smallest farmers, had gradually become a generalized problem, defying any ability to redress the situation. The indebted peasants were threatened with lawsuits, or were already involved in them, and risked losing their land.

> *In June and July 2010, that is, several months before the fall and departure of Ben Ali, farmers from Regueb and Sidi Bouzid demonstrated in front of the governorate building against the lawsuits brought against them by the BNA (Banque Nationale Agricole) and the processes of judicial liquidation aimed against them. About 20 debtor families whose properties had been liquidated organized sit-ins on their lands to oppose their expropriation. Later, a protest march was organized in front of the governorate building, which was brutally dispersed by the police forces.* (Gana 2012:3)

Among the dozens, even hundreds, of demonstrators, several accounts consistent with each other, collected in my many trips around the region, suggest that Muhammad Bouazizi was present at these demonstrations and sit-ins; however, his presence could not be verified. In any event, the connection between these peasant 'mobilizations' of summer 2010 and those that followed Bouazizi's desperate act[17] seems obvious to me. It explains why this particular suicide, unlike others, set off the solidarity movement that transformed so rapidly into the massive popular uprising that began in Sidi Bouzid on December 17, spread throughout the center and the south of the country, and ended on Avenue Bourguiba in Tunis in the "monster" demonstration of January 14, 2011.

This is unquestionably a case of class solidarity (Hopkins 1983) on the part of the inhabitants of the region[18] directly affected, like Bouazizi, by the numerous local economic and social troubles,

---

17 These demonstrations involved, in particular, hundreds of young people in the region. Many of these were the sons of impoverished peasants, who felt excluded from the 'agricultural development' that they could see but could not benefit from; they had lost all hope for their future. See the film *Mezzouna, après la chute* (Romain André, Élisa Le Briand, Anna Saint-Araille, and Saber Zammouri, 85 min., 2014).

18 The population of the region is largely rural. Even in the town of Sidi Bouzid, about 70 percent of the population is engaged in activities connected with the farming sector (farmers, farm workers, seasonal farm workers, etc.).

including limited access to land and other agricultural resources, as discussed above, and the various processes of dispossession suffered by the local peasantry. For a few days, this class solidarity could be seen throughout the country, beginning in the rural zones (including the rural towns), before it reached the lower-class neighborhoods of the larger towns and, finally, the big urban centers. The progress of this protest movement between December 17, 2010 and January 14, 2011, as well as that of the longer revolutionary process (January 2008–January 2011; see fig. 1), gives evidence of a certain class consciousness that actually goes beyond the peasantry to reach the entire rural and urban population. The evolution of the farming sector in Sidi Bouzid will demonstrate the extent of these changes.

The Green Mirage of Sidi Bouzid: "Confiscated" Lands, Lands in Revolt

If there is a region in Tunisia where the mechanisms of accumulation by dispossession (Harvey 2004) are more flagrant and visible than elsewhere, it is undeniably the region of Sidi Bouzid, situated in the arid plain in the center of the country, which even in good years receives barely 250 millimeters of rain annually.[19] It is a steppe region, historically inhabited by a population that has traditionally practiced semi-nomadic pastoralism and extensive rainfed agriculture. The raising of sheep and camels, and the cultivation of olive trees, almond trees, and seasonal grains (chiefly barley), constitute the principal agricultural activities.

Irrigated agricultural land in the Sidi Bouzid governorate increased from 2,000 hectares in 1958 to 8,700 in 1974, 21,000 in 1987, 25,000 in 1993, and 47,000 in 2011 (Ayeb 2013). Currently this amounts to 10% of the usable agricultural land in the region, thanks to the growing role of capital from outside the governorate in the harnessing of water for irrigation, especially in the Regueb region (22%).

Yet in less than three decades, Sidi Bouzid became one of the primary agricultural regions of the country, and the first in certain products, such as vegetables. Within this region, the irrigated sector now accounts for 50% of the total production (irrigated plus non-irrigated land), and 10% to 15% of the national market-gardening production. The region has become the country's primary vegetable

---

19 Overall, Tunisia is rainy in the north, dry in the center, and desert in the south.

producer and one of its principal dairy producers.[20] There are three tomato-drying firms producing solely for the export market—SODAF, HTF, and AGRIT—as well as three firms for processing tomatoes and harissa, for both local consumption and export. Its contribution to the total agricultural production of the country is impressive: 13.8% of its olives, 13% of its almonds, 20% of its pistachios, 18% of its vegetables, and 7% of its red meats. A few additional figures will show the variety of Sidi Bouzid's agricultural production (in tons per year): milk, 56,000; oils, 51,500; market gardening, 490,000 (on a total area of 16,000 hectares); grains (irrigated), 41,000; almonds, 7,850. Livestock includes 17,500 head of cows, 350,000 of sheep, and 51,000 of goats. Eighteen collection and processing centers process about 90% of the regional milk production. These figures show the extent of the disruption caused by the current agricultural policies. While traditionally, milk was primarily for home consumption and its sale was viewed as degrading, it is now mainly destined for the urban market (Jouili, Kahouli, and Elloumi 2011).

Because of the growing demand for agricultural land in certain sectors of the region, notably in Regueb, the town of Menzel Bouzaiane (in the Sidi Bouzid region) has seen the development of a dynamic real-estate market, which has caused real-estate prices to rise sharply. As a result, only investors with access to considerable financial means, acquired elsewhere, can afford the costs of any new intensive agriculture project based on irrigation: the purchase of land, the drilling of wells, equipment, electrification, irrigation networks, plantations (Daoud and Trautmann 1997). They are the only ones in a position not only to acquire the land, but above all to set up highly intensive, mechanized, and profitable agricultural projects.

At first sight, the Sidi Bouzid region looks like what one could call the "Silicon Valley" or the "Little California" of Tunisian agriculture. The uninformed traveler who visits the region for the first time would find it difficult to imagine the scale of the changes that have taken place over the last 30 or 35 years. The green landscapes everywhere, especially in the Regueb district, would lead one to believe that the region suffers no shortage of water resources. The intense

---

20 It also produces, and sells commercially, a breed of lamb raised locally that has obtained an AOC ('appellation d'origine contrôlée') label.

level of agriculture and irrigation, visible for several kilometers along local roads, gives a false idea of the natural and financial wealth of the area. The whole "front view" of the countryside suggests that the region has impressive capacities and, thus, has produced its own large-scale investors. But even the most superficial investigation of the terrain shows that this entire first impression is totally baseless. In Sidi Bouzid there are neither great native financial riches, nor large local investors.

The truth is an "optical distortion" of the local realities, dominated by the relative scarcity of local natural resources[21] and by the absence of large holders of capital who are native to the region. Even though underground water is relatively abundant, the fact remains that it is provided by aquifers that are barely renewable or non-renewable. It is in danger of being depleted rapidly if its current exploitation by drilling continues and intensifies in the coming years—a situation which, unfortunately, is now being confirmed. Already, irrigation water—and even drinking water—shows a relatively high level of salinization, which reflects, among other factors, the dropping level of the water table and the slowness of its natural rate of replenishment. "The many incentives for the practice of irrigation and the spectacular proliferation of wells and drillings have led to overexploitation of the water tables." The reserves of underground water are diminishing, and "the dropping [of the water table] has in some places reached several meters, causing the intrusion of salt water from the edges of the table" (Daoud and Trautmann 1997:4).

Furthermore, the dynamics of farming, and particularly of the real-estate market, since the years 1980–1990, and the strong and rapid extension of intensive irrigated agriculture, have not helped the Sidi Bouzid governorate to climb out of the poverty zone that covers the entire central-west region of the country, where the poverty rates rose to more than 32.3% in 2010, compared to 9.1% for Greater Tunis, 10.3% for the northeast, and 8.0% for the center-east (INS 2012:16).

---

21 The notion of scarcity, with respect to natural resources, especially water, is very vague and does not give a precise idea of the qualitative and quantitative availability of the resource. It particularly emphasizes the disjuncture between availability of the resource and the means of exploitation directed toward it. 'Scarcity' is thus invented, not natural. By all evidence, there will never be enough water to make the Sahara bloom.

According to the Ministry of Social Affairs, the poverty rates are even higher in the Sidi Bouzid region: 42.3% in 2011, versus 13.4% for Tunis and the national average of 24%[22] (Touhami 2012:7; Bechir and Sghaier 2013:7–8).

The capital comes, essentially, from the Sahel (the coastal cities on the country's east coast), and more specifically from the city of Sfax, which is the closest big city, and from Tunis. When they are not exported directly outside the country, products are transported to the markets of Tunis and other cities in the north and the Sahel, or else to the processing plants, mainly in Sfax (for olives to be pressed into olive oil, which is largely exported) and in Cap Bon (for tomatoes to be processed into tomato concentrates, also partly exported).

The example of the Sidi Bouzid region alone demonstrates, as if it were necessary, that economic growth, measured strictly on a financial and accounting basis, is not at all incompatible with the growth of poverty and the worsening of the various processes that (re)produce it. Here, as just about everywhere else in Tunisia and in the world, it is not completely unfounded to assert that this kind of economic growth can actually contribute to the aggravation and the reproduction of poverty, unless it is systematically corrected by apposite measures developed and put in place directly by the state.

Thus the investors, 'foreigners' in the region, exploit the local resources (water and land) for production that only marginally benefits the local population and the region—amounting to a few jobs, relatively modest in number because most of the employees come from other regions, and the local fruit and vegetable markets. Obviously, the smallholders, who practice extensive traditional agriculture, can neither follow the trend of massive investment, nor protect their resources (especially water, whose underground exploitation they cannot prevent) and their own production, nor long resist the real-estate market, which nibbles away at their land and progressively excludes them from the agricultural sector.

---

22 To measure poverty, the Social Services office of the Ministry of Social Affairs (MAS) draws data from various types of social services: low-income, social aid (reduced-rate cards for various services, beneficiaries of alimony guarantees, disabled persons, at-risk youth, etc.), and PNAFN recipients (Programme national d'aide aux familles nécessiteuses, or welfare).

The False Miracle of Sidi Bouzid: Modernism, Irrigationalism, and Liberalism

Far from being a miracle, the case of Sidi Bouzid is merely a reflection of a process of accumulation, to the benefit of some, by dispossession, to the detriment of others. It is a green mirage that quickly disappears as soon as one looks more closely to analyze what is being concealed by the figures that make the decision-makers, the experts, and of course the investors so proud, but that expose a mechanical process of social exclusion of the local population.

At the origin of the green miracle of Sidi Bouzid can be found the famous "irrigation ideology" as an agricultural development model based on the full mobilization of water resources to create an agricultural sector that is strongly intensive, capitalist, and export-oriented (Blake 2012).[23] This is the line that was taken by the colonial power well before independence, and then taken up and confirmed by the independent Tunisian state.

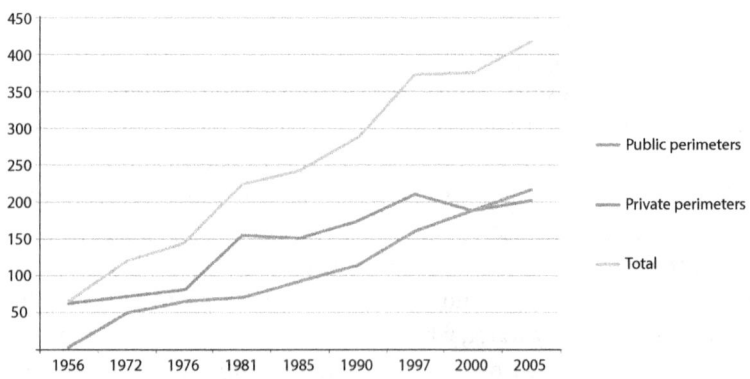

Fig. 2. Change in land area under irrigation (1000 hectares) (Source: Author, from statistical data of FAOSTAT)

---

23 Irrigation ideology can be summed up by a set of ideas and conceptual tools that lend a discursive and technical coherence to development policies based on the mobilization and mastery of water resources in the service of a developmentalist project conceived and managed by the state or by some other central, more or less authoritarian, power and its reigning experts.

Thus, Tunisia's postcolonial development policy was initiated, and has been pursued, under successive formulas and adjustments, often connected to political 'evolutions,' but systematically under the label of 'modernity' and technical modernization that constituted the very foundation of Bourguiba's political project,[24] which aimed to create a 'modern' and 'open' economy in the world market. In practice, it has been expressed by the choice of modern techniques and technologies such as dams, deep drilling, water-transfer networks among regions, the mechanization of agriculture and irrigation, and the introduction of new water-management technologies and techniques.

In the service of this policy, several tools are brought to bear: obligatory registration of farmland,[25] liberalization of the markets in land, water, credits, inputs (chemical fertilizers, pesticides, and insecticides), and trade patterns, as well as the orientation of the state's efforts to give first priority to agribusiness. The aim is to incorporate agriculture into 'food security' and into the country's balance of trade.

One of the most visible dimensions of this voluntarist modernization policy has incontestably been the widespread use of irrigation, wherever possible, and the extension of irrigated land into the deserts and steppes, particularly around the oases and in the central and southern regions of the country. The total irrigated area in Tunisia has grown from around 60,000 hectares in the 1960s to around 500,000 hectares today—a ninefold increase in about 50 years (see fig. 2). A technical success, to be sure, but one that nevertheless conceals considerable economic, social, and environmental consequences. Intended to improve the export capacity of the farm sector, the expansion of

---

24 "To draw from the soil or land the things she can give us, we need to take advantage of modern techniques...the example of the former French settlers is there to instruct us." Habib Bourguiba, speech delivered in 1964 at Tozeur (southwestern Tunisia).

25 A law on real estate promulgated on July 1, 1885 (four years after the beginning of the French occupation) introduced the system of real-estate registration, in French the *cadastre*, which consists in regularizing the legal status of land and recognizes the property rights of the applicant. Its chief object was to facilitate the access of European settlers to farmland. French colonization adopted, for its African colonies, the Torrens law or system ("Torrens Act"), named for the English colonel Robert Torrens, who instituted the system of real-estate records in Australia in 1858. Now in effect in most countries, the cadastre or land registry at first permitted the dispossession of indigenous populations in the colonies. Even today, the registry requirement has the effect of privatizing collective (tribal or family) land.

irrigation has greatly modified the agricultural landscape—water-related as well as social—with the appearance of new forms of social and geographic marginality.

In the Gabes region, it is estimated that between the 1980s and the present, the amount of traditionally watered land (i.e., by oasis) has been reduced by half, while the total irrigated land has doubled (Ayeb 2014). A particularly rich natural heritage of biodiversity is in the process of disappearing forever. The oasis peasantry has been destructured, marginalized, and deprived of its resources, including land and water. An environment has been dangerously degraded by the combination of diminished availability of water resources and the effects of pollution caused by the chemical industry set up in the early 1970s right on the edge of the palm grove. These are only a few of the items on the dramatic list of the modernization policy imposed all over the country, especially in the agricultural sector, without taking the least account of local knowledge, the local ecological and environmental wealth, and the food needs of nearly half a million peasant families, and indeed of the entire population.

Earlier, one finds the sacrosanct paradigm of food security,[26] which the Fifth Tunisian Five-Year Plan (1977–1981), created after the abandonment of collectivism,[27] defined as follows: "The objective assigned to the agricultural and fishing sector is to attain, by 1981, food self-sufficiency, to be accomplished by means of the balance of

---

26 Dating from the end of the 1940s, and running counter to the idea of food self-sufficiency, which was neither realistic nor realizable, the concept of food security was carved in stone and became the food objective at which every country should aim. This concept refers to the ability of a country to assure an adequate diet for its entire population, via either production or acquisition (purchases or donated food aid). Nevertheless, the concept of 'food security' does not necessarily mean that every citizen has permanent, secure access to an amount of food that is adequate in both quantity and quality. Thus, the principal measure of food security is the balance of trade. It is this liberal vision that, even today, rules the agricultural policies of many countries of the global South, including Tunisia.

27 Between 1962 and 1969, Tunisia launched an experiment in collectivization of the means of production, including farmland. Also known as a 'socialist' or 'cooperativist' experiment, this policy was conducted by Ahmed Ben Salah, a powerful former minister, with the blessing of President Habib Bourguiba and the PSD (Parti Socialist Destourien), which turned against him in 1969. This experiment, which did not include large landowners, had a dramatic effect on smallholders, whose current problems are a direct result of the consequences of this experiment.

trade in foodstuffs." Reinforcing this definition, the Sixth and Seventh Plans (1987–1996) specified that "the role of agriculture is to contribute to the external balance of trade, a balanced public budget, balanced employment, and balance among regions." These functions and objectives for the agricultural sector were confirmed by the Agricultural Structural Adjustment Plan (Plan d'Adjustement Structurel Agricole [PASA]) adopted by Tunisia in 1987, under pressure from the World Bank and the IMF.

The very rapid development of the irrigated agricultural sector in Sidi Bouzid arose from this same logic and the same overall strategies. The selection of this region to serve as a new center for irrigated agriculture, principally export-oriented, did not happen by chance. It was based on a certain 'technicist' and 'economistic' perception of the local geographic and social realities, as well as the economic and political ones. First, the region was viewed as an "empty" space, whose natural resources (including water and land) were being badly and insufficiently exploited—hence the need to mobilize them to the benefit of the national economy.[28] Second, the economic—rather, 'economistic'—vision at work here failed to take the long view. The goal was not tomorrow, but today, hence the need to massively exploit the current resources in order to produce measurable growth, sacrificing future generations in favor of current users. Third, the Mafia-like power of the dictatorship had its clients, who had to be enriched. Water and land had to serve, above all, the investors who were seeking good placements, profits, speculations, and returns. Encouraging them to go and pillage the resources of Sidi Bouzid would be good for both sides: it would augment the country's export capacities and the state revenues, while also increasing the investors' profits. Fourth, the supposed—invented, actually—"emptiness" of Sidi Bouzid and of the entire center of the country was considered not just demographic, but financial as well, due to the absence of "real" capital, and of large capitalists and investors, in the region. It was thus viewed as an attractive region for Tunisian and foreign investors, who could set up or dismantle their

---

28 During the colonial period in Tunisia, as elsewhere, the "empty space" argument was often used, including by some people who called themselves anticolonialists, in order to justify what were called "population colonies." Even the libertarian and anticolonialist geographer Elisée Reclus (1830–1905) justified this colonization project in Sudan and the Sahara, on the grounds that these were empty spaces, which rendered their occupation, including occupation by foreign powers, legitimate and even useful.

agricultural projects without any risk of strong local competition. They would thus enjoy an exclusive monopoly, from which they could derive considerable profits. This is, in a way, what David Harvey calls "monopoly profit" ("*la rente du monopole*") (Harvey 2008). In effect, the simple fact that the 'foreign' investors held the monopoly on the water resources of the aquifers in Sidi Bouzid meant that they not only received the profits from their investments; they also enjoyed material and symbolic benefits. This explains, at least partially, why investors who are Tunisian but not from the region are called 'foreigners' or 'settlers'[29] by the local peasants, and regarded as invaders.

The mobilization of resources and the expansion of irrigated lands have fostered a true agricultural dynamism in the region, but the local producers, including those who have converted to irrigated agriculture, do not enjoy the same favors and encouragement. They have "experienced a crisis and a process of exclusion from irrigation, and farms of 5 to 10 hectares lack financial means" (Jouili, Kahouli, and Elloumi 2011). They are increasingly exposed to the risk of losing their individual or collective lands, which they have often inherited and which constitute their sole social and material capital. For them, the loss of land is a loss of resources, but even more a loss of social status and thus of their dignity. When the demonstrators of December 17, 2010–January 14, 2011 were chanting "Bread, social justice, and dignity," they were also referring to the loss of the status that land and water provided them.

By means of these processes of accumulation by dispossession, the peasants, who are far from being statistically insignificant and who, by virtue of their numbers, play a major role in local and national 'food security,' find themselves progressively marginalized. Their economic and social marginalization has reached such a level that they have become almost totally invisible and inaudible. But by their resistance and their acts of protest, including during the rule of Ben Ali, the peasants have demonstrated an unshakable attachment to their land and their resources, as a priceless symbolic inheritance, as social and economic capital, and as a guarantee of

---

29 The term 'settler,' which in Tunisia refers to the French during the occupation, is used in Latin America to designate the 'planters' who clear the Amazon forest in order to create plantations.

food 'security'—even if relative—on the family and local scale, for themselves and for future generations.

The following extract from an interview conducted during my research in the Gabes Oasis in the southeast, with a peasant whom we shall call Ahmad, who describes himself as a "poor peasant," shows his attachment to the land.

Me:	What should I call you? Fellah (peasant)?
Ahmad:	I am a fellah, son of a fellah, and grandson of a fellah.
Me:	Do you live exclusively from your land?
Ahmad:	No, of course not. I have barely a quarter hectare. Fortunately I find odd jobs here and there, otherwise my children would starve.
Me:	Do you consider yourselves poor?
Ahmad:	We are more than poor. We don't live. We don't exist.
Me:	If I offered you a good price, would you agree to sell me your plot?
Ahmad:	Never. [long silence] Sell you my parents' land? My grandparents' land? My children's land? I'll never sell this land. I was born here, I'll die here, and I'll be buried not far from here.
Me:	But with the money you could provide capital for your children.
Ahmad:	This land is priceless. It isn't for sale. It's a kind of capital that can't be equaled.

Those who think they see a lack of economic 'rationality' in the words of my interlocutor should perhaps consider that the peasant, exceptionally poor, might have a peasant sense of rationality—the rationality of the daily struggle for survival and dignity, so often ignored by certain academic analyses.

Even before January 2008, in several regions, peasants with and without land took some particularly spectacular action, even though their isolation, particularly from the media, facilitated the repressive work of the police who encountered them. For some years, the peasants had refused to pay their electricity and water bills and to repay the BNA loans. But their most spectacular action was the "illegal" occupation, by smallholders and landless peasants, of farmland belonging to the state. As an example, in 1997, 150 families occupied about 400 hectares of state land, located near the Gabes chemical complex (Ayeb 2014). Severe repression, the arrests of entire families, trials and imprisonment, could not make these "squatter" peasants bend. These types of collective action, better known in Latin America and Asia, unquestionably constitute acts of resistance against agricultural policies that deny them access to land and water, as well as to other material and political resources: subsidies, guaranteed prices, insurance, bank credits, markets.

Conclusion

Two important conclusions can be drawn from the preceding discussion. The first is that, contrary to the current theses about 'revolution' in Tunisia, and more broadly on the processes of social change in the Tunisian countryside, peasants' problems and broader agricultural, food, and rural issues occupy a large place in the revolutionary processes that led to the fall of the Ben Ali dictatorship on January 14, 2011. By accelerating the processes of marginalization of the peasantry and the rural population, the mechanisms of accumulation by dispossession, encouraged by the state, automatically fed the processes of resistance and challenge. The unhappy story of Muhammad Bouazizi, in itself, summarizes and symbolizes both the processes of marginalization and exclusion, and the processes of resistance and challenge.

The second conclusion that can be proposed is that the unleashing of massive mobilization, beginning on December 17, 2010, can be explained in large part by a form of class solidarity on the part of the Sidi Bouzid peasantry in the face of the loss of one of their own. This supports the thesis that, far from being a simple, spontaneous revolt inspired by collective emotion in reaction to a dramatic item of "miscellaneous news," the revolution in Tunisia and in other countries in the region forms part of the long and complex "underground" revolutionary processes that the dictatorship and its neoliberal policies involuntarily and unconsciously fed and encouraged.

These two conclusions, it seems to me, demonstrate the relevance of "socio-spatial classes" as the principal point of entry for analyzing and understanding the deep upheavals that, even today, are shaking the societies of the states in the region and even beyond.

References

Ayeb, H. 2010. *Crise de la société rurale en Egypte: La fin du fellah?* Paris: Karthala.

———. 2011. "Social and Political Geography of the Tunisian Revolution: The Alfa Grass Revolution," *Review of African Political Economy*, 38(129): 467–479.

———. 2012. "Competitions over Resources and Small Farmers' Marginalization in Egypt and Tunisia." In R. Bush and H. Ayeb, eds., *Marginality and Exclusion in Egypt*, 72–96. London: Zed Books. Arabic version published by Dar al-Ayn, Cairo.

———.2013."Le Rural Dans la Révolution en Tunisie: les voix inaudibles" in *Demmer* (blog). https://habibayeb.wordpress.com/2013/09/28/le-rural-dans-la-revolution-en-tunisie-les-voix-inaudibles/

———. 2014. *Gabes Labess* [All is Well in Gabes]. Documentary. 47 min. Amaru (France) and 5/5 (Tunisia) Productions.

Ayeb, H., and R. Bush. 2014. "Small Farmer Uprisings and Rural Neglect in Egypt and Tunisia," *Middle East Research and Information Project*, no. 272, 44(3) Autumn. http://www.merip.org/mer/mer272/small-farmer-uprisings-rural-neglect-egypt-tunisia

Bechir, R., and M. Sghaier. 2013. "Taux de pauvreté et ses mesures en Tunisie," *New Médit*, 12(2): 2–10.

Blake, D. J. H. 2012. "Irrigationalism: The Politics and Ideology of Irrigation Development in the Nam Songkhram Basin, Northeast Thailand." PhD diss., University of East Anglia. https://ueaeprints.uea.ac.uk/47934/1/2012BlakeDJHPhD.pdf

CDCGE. 2014. "Plan d'action régional de lutte contre la désertification du gouvernorat de Sidi Bouzid."Consulting en Développement Communautaire et en Gestion d'Entreprise (CDCGE). http://www.environnement.nat.tn/sid/dmdocuments/mise_oeuvre/parlcd/parlcd_sidibouzid.pdf

Daoud, A. 2001. "La révolution tunisienne de janvier 2011: une lecture par les déséquilibres du territoire," *EchoGéo*, Septembre: 2–13.

Daoud, A., and J. Trautmann. 1997. "Rôle de la télédétection dans l'évaluation et la cartographie des épandages artificiels des crues dans les hautes steppes tunisiennes." In *Télédétection et ressources en eau*. Actes de l'atelier international, Montpellier, France, 30 november–1 décembre 1995. 1, 1995. http://horizon.documentation.ird.fr/exl-doc/pleins_textes/divers12-08/010004787.pdf

Friedmann, H. 1982. "The Political Economy of Food: The Rise and Fall of the Postwar International Food Order," *American Journal of Sociology*, 88S: 248–286.

———. 1987. "International Regimes of Food and Agriculture since 1870." In T. Shanin, ed., *Peasants and Peasant Societies*, 258–276. Oxford: Basil Blackwell.

———. 1993. "The Political Economy of Food: A Global Crisis," *New Left Review*, 197: 29–57.

———. 1994. "Distance and Durability: Shaky Foundations of the World Food Economy." In P. McMichael, ed., *The Global Restructuring of Agro-Food Systems*, 371–383. Ithaca, NY: Cornell University Press.

Friedmann, H., and P. McMichael. 1989. "Agriculture and the State System: The Rise and Decline of National Agriculture from 1870 to the Present," *Sociologia Ruralis*, 14: 93–118.

Gana, A. 2012. "Agriculteurs et paysans: nouveaux acteurs de la société civile et de la transition démocratique en Tunisie?" L'Observatoire Tunisien de la Transition Démocratique (OTTD). http://www.observatoireTunisien.org/index.php?swt=01&id=28

Harvey, D. 2004. "The 'New' Imperialism: Accumulation by Dispossession," *Socialist Register*, 40: 63–87.

———. 2008. *Géographie de la domination*. Paris: Les Prairies Ordinaires.

Hopkins, N. S. 1983. *Testour, ou la transformation des campagnes maghrébines*. Tunis: Cérès Productions.

INS (Institut National de la Statistique). 2012. "Mesure de la pauvreté, des inégalités et de la polarisation en Tunisie 2000–2010, à partir des données collectées lors de l'Enquête Nationale sur le Budget, la Consommation et le Niveau de Vie des ménages conduite en 2010–2011." Tunis: INS.

Jouili, M., I. Kahouli, and M. Elloumi. 2011. "Libéralisation de l'accès aux ressources hydrauliques et processus d'exclusion au niveau du gouvernorat de Sidi Bouzid (Tunisie Centrale)." In *Appropriation des ressources naturelles et patrimoniales: compétitions et droits d'accès en Méditerranée*. Colloque ESG–Méditerranée. Beyrouth, les 28–29–30 Novembre.

Lassudrie-Duchêne, B., and D. Ünal-Kesenci. 2001. "L'avantage comparatif, notion fondamentale et controversée." In *L'Economie Mondiale 2002*, 90–104. Repères. Paris: La Découverte.

Saad, R. 2002. "Egyptian Politics and the Tenancy Law." In R. Bush, ed., *Counter Revolution in Egypt's Countryside*, 103–125. London: Zed Books.

Touhami, H. 2012. "Seuil de Pauvreté, Population Pauvre." Conférence donnée le 7 mars 2012 à la Faculté des Sciences Economiques de Tunis à l'invitation du Club des Econométres Tunisiens. http://www.leaders.com.tn/uploads/FCK_files/file/SEUIL%20DE%20PAUVRETE-VDF-Leaders.pdf

CHAPTER 7

Reflection on the Concept of Hunger: The Case of Egypt between 2008 and 2010

Malak S. Rouchdy

As early as the second half of 2011, and after the January 25 Revolution in that year, Egyptian officials and the media gave warnings about the potential eruption of what they called "the revolts of the hungry," if political violence and economic crisis were to persist. In their speeches and discourses, they depicted images of the revolts of the hungry that were reminiscent of the bread riots of January 1977, which seem to have been haunting Egyptian officials as well as international organizations ever since. For example, the International Food Policy Research Institute (IFPRI) (Breisinger et al. 2013) and the World Food Program (WFP) (IDSC 2013) have published several reports over the last few years assessing the food situation in Egypt in relation to poverty, political instability, and hunger.

In this chapter, I would like to revisit the concept of hunger as used by Egyptian officials and UN agencies, from 2008 until 2010. This period coincides with the beginning of the food crisis in Egypt, which erupted with the beginning of the global food crisis. It also corresponds to the expansion of contentious politics, the intensification of the confrontations between the workers' movements and the state, and the development of social political movements. In fact, it was the beginning of the end of Mubarak's authoritarian regime.

The food crisis and the effects of its spillover pushed the regime to look for leeway to alleviate economic pressures on the population and pre-empt riots and uprisings. The government and UN agencies embarked on an assessment of the situation, reaching the conclusion that a considerable segment of the society was at risk of food deprivation. Based on these findings, UN organizations referred the causes behind the local food crisis to the global one, but equally to the inability of policy makers to implement adequately the directives of food security policies as agreed upon between the Egyptian officials and international agencies.

It is in this context that I will first examine how official perceptions of hunger and food deprivation are constructed, and how the construction of the discourse around hunger attempted to justify the actions and the practices of politicians and policy makers in this situation. This will be followed by an analysis of the ways in which the term 'hunger' has been put to political and social use. In a second part, I will explore how and why the discourse around the crisis management, and the justifications advanced by the government, the international organizations, and the corporate institutions, ultimately led to the appropriation of the word by its users and the de-politicization of the term 'hunger.'

Alarming Voices

Early in 2008, the international press reported that Egypt, like many countries in the world, was facing a severe food crisis that was leading a considerable segment of the population into food deprivation. Reporters emphasized the danger behind the political implications of the crisis, particularly that the country had become the site of contentious politics, civil society protests, and workers' strikes.[1] Food shortages, particularly bread, led countless numbers of people to queue for endless hours in front of bakeries hoping to buy a few loaves. Concomitant to the food shortages, Egypt saw the beginning of a long series of workers' strikes and civil society movements protesting Mubarak's authoritarian regime. These were the movements that gradually paved the way to the January 2011 uprisings. What is equally worth mentioning is the important international media coverage that the workers' strike had earned,

---

1 *The Telegraph*, "Egyptians Riot over Bread Crisis," April 8, 2008, http://www.telegraph.co.uk/finance/economics/2787714/Egyptians-riot-over-bread-crisis.html; BBC News, "Egypt Army to Tackle Bread Crisis," March 17, 2008, http://news.bbc.co.uk/2/hi/middle_east/7300899.stm; Ulrike Putz, "The Daily Struggle for Food," *Spiegel Online*, April 18, 2008, http://www.spiegel.de/international/world/crisis-in-egypt-the-daily-struggle-for-food-a-548300.html

particularly in the cities of Mahalla al-Kubra and Mansura.[2] The images and the reports that were circulating at the time showed the important magnitude of the strikes, and the strong determination on the part of workers to continue their struggle. It was amid these political entanglements that the term 'hunger' emerged in the official public discourse to describe a very particular social crisis, the food crisis, in isolation from the overall sociopolitical conflicts.[3]

During the same year, Reuters reported that around 11 people died from heart attacks queuing at local markets to buy bread,[4] and the BBC News reported that Hosni Mubarak issued a presidential order to the ministries of Defense and Interior to distribute bread to the people as a measure to alleviate the sociopolitical pressures of the food crisis on the population.[5] The events came as a tragedy to public opinion, particularly since there is a common-sense understanding in Egypt that "no one ever starves to death."[6] This belief is partly related to the assumption that resources will be sufficient if social solidarity prevails through charity and 'gifts.'[7] Shortly thereafter, the WFP, in cooperation with the Egyptian government and GAIN (Global Alliance for Improved Nutrition), provided around 11 million Egyptians with more nutritious bread, reaching 45 million people by 2010.[8] Classifying Egypt as a country facing hunger

2 Mansura and Mahalla are two industrial cities in the northeast of the Delta.
3 Libcom.org, "Ghazl el-Mahalla Riots, Egypt, April 6–7, 2008," April 16, 2008, http://libcom.org/gallery/ghazl-el-mahalla-riots-egypt-april-6-7th-2008; Joel Beinin, "Egypt: Bread Riots and Mill Strikes," *Le Monde diplomatique*, May 2008, http://mondediplo.com/2008/05/08egypt
4 Cynthia Johnston, "In Egypt, Long Queues for Bread That's Almost Free," April 6, 2008, http://www.reuters.com/article/us-agflation-subsidies-idUSL0404033220080406
5 BBC News, "Egypt's Army to Tackle Bread Crisis." It should be noted that the Ministry of Defense and the Ministry of Interior own and control numerous large bakeries for the supply of their troops.
6 Chris McGreal, "Egypt: Bread Shortages, Hunger and Unrest," *The Guardian*, May 27, 2008, https://www.theguardian.com/environment/2008/may/27/food.egypt
7 The term 'gift' refers to the very broad definition developed by Marcel Mauss. For him the 'gift' is a multidimensional phenomenon in which various social structures enter into its formulation as codes and practices. The concept of 'gift' has among its dimensions the dimension of obligation and return, or a form of 'coded reciprocity' (Mauss 1980:150–151).
8 Marc van Ameringen, "Egypt: Launch of More Nutritious Vegetable Oil," Global Alliance for Improved Nutrition (GAIN), October 30, 2010, http://www.gainhealth.org/knowledge-centre/egypt-launch-nutritious-vegetable-oil/

fostered the government's efforts and resulted in a big media promotion announcing the launching of an international march, under the auspices of Ms. Suzanne Mubarak, the WFP, and TNT Express Co., for fund raising and as an awareness campaign to combat starvation and hunger. The event took place on June 1, 2008 in the gated gardens of the Smart Village, located on the Cairo–Alexandria Desert Road.[9] The march included about 800 figures from the government, the media, and movie stars. The campaign was repeated two years later, in June 2010, with approximately 1,000 public figures attending and participating in the event.[10] This time the march took place on the newly constructed campus of the American University in Cairo, a gated establishment located in the vast desert of the New Cairo residential area. From behind the guarded walls of AUC and those of the Smart Village, and through the deployment of the military and the police for bread production and distribution, the government, the corporate community, and the WFP thought to have contributed publicly and from a distance to the crisis, without, however, directly addressing the 'hungry' or those who were suffering from food scarcity. The concerned subjects, the 'hungry,' were mentioned during this crisis in the passive voice, and they were referred to in aggregate figures and statistics. The only protagonists in this story and in the official discourse were the policy makers and their supporters, who remained the only actors to speak on behalf of the 'hungry,' the voiceless.

In general, the regime presented the local food crisis as a direct consequence of the sweeping wave of rising global food and fuel prices. Hunger was thus perceived as the spillover of the international food market crisis. In the meantime, Egypt's population had to face international increases in food prices as high as 54 percent over one year, as per FAO (Food and Agricultural Organization) estimates in 2008. The official message on this crisis was clear and concise: under such global circumstances, even an economy witnessing unprecedented 7 percent growth would not be able to avoid food scarcity and hunger. Egypt had to face its destiny! The government explained rightly that

---

9 *al-Akhbar*, "WFP," May 19, 2008, http://ar.wfp.org/news/news-release/4653. The Smart Village was built in 2000. It is a complex of business, service, conference, and administrative centers constructed on 182 hectares and includes technological incubators to support businesses in the field of technology.

10 *al-Akhbar*, "WFP," May 31, 2010, http://ar.wfp.org/news/news-release/13121

the crisis was the consequence of several conjunctures in the global markets, notably the increasing demand for biofuel production,[11] the bad weather conditions in food-producing countries, and the decline in global food stocks due to international market forces.[12] The government's analysis was based on the OECD-FAO *Agricultural Outlook 2008–2017* report (OECD 2008),[13] which offered important insights on the global food crisis and demonstrated how market forces, economic interests, and climatic changes converge at times and threaten world food supplies. However, policy makers failed to acknowledge that global economic conditions could not have been solely responsible for Egypt's food and agricultural crisis.

Background of the Food Crisis
It will be relevant to examine the discourse of the development agencies in their assessment of Egypt's economic performance and business environment prior to the food crisis, for it will shed light on the role they played in the development of the crisis, the emergence of food shortages on a large scale, and the exacerbation of poverty rates.

Throughout the 2000s, the Mubarak regime pursued the Economic Reforms and Structural Adjustment Policies plans (ERSAP) as agreed upon with the World Bank and the IMF in the 1990s. Among the numerous measures they agreed upon were the expansion of the free-market economy on a large scale, and the reduction of state subsidies on food items and agricultural inputs. As a result, the ERSAP agreement led to the growth of the free markets, the withdrawal of the state from many economic sectors, the proliferation of the activities of businessmen, the expansion of the private sector, and the heavy involvement of the latter in

---

11 Second-generation biofuels, also known as advanced biofuels, are fuels that can be manufactured from various types of biomass. Biomass is a wide-ranging term covering any source of organic carbon that is renewed rapidly as part of the carbon cycle. Biomass is mainly derived from plant materials but can also include animal materials. First-generation biofuels are made from the sugars and vegetable oils found in food crops, which can be easily extracted using conventional technology. In comparison, second-generation biofuels are made from lignocellulosic biomass or woody crops, agricultural residues, or waste, from which it is harder to extract the fuel. For more information, see OECD-FAO 2008.

12 Nader Noureldin, "The New Face of Hunger," *Al-Ahram Weekly*, September 4–10, 2008.

13 OECD is the Organisation for Economic Co-operation and Development.

state politics. Thus, a new emerging business elite took the lead in food imports serving one of the largest expanding markets in Egypt: food packaging and food distribution. Further, the changes in the economic policies meant a change in the balance of political power; for the first time and in an unprecedented development, the businessmen who became close to the ruling elite dominated the newly elected parliament in 2005, and a small group of Muslim Brothers who were both technocrats and heads of commercial enterprises won a number of parliamentary seats, also for the first time (Blaydes 2011:53–55). The parliament introduced a series of legislation to allow free markets to operate efficiently, and amended the constitution in 2007 to recognize the power of the free markets and their role in the Egyptian state, while removing references to the Nasserite state, as indicated in the fourth article of the 1971 Constitution.[14] On another level, by 2006, the real GDP growth rate had increased considerably, to reach 6.5%, and the budget deficit was reduced from 15% in 1991 to 8.2%. By 2007, Egypt was ranked the top country in the world for achieving reforms and improving its business environment. However, the praises of the international organizations could not conceal for long the underlying sociopolitical and economic deficiencies of the regime, to the point that Egypt was ranked 105 out of 169 countries on the Corruption Perception Index in the same year (Sufyan 2007:7, 18–19).[15]

What appears paradoxical, in the narrative of the examined reports, is the flagrant contradiction between the praise that international organizations offered to the achievements of the Egyptian government for its overall macroeconomic policies and their unconditional support of the regime, and their insistence on revealing aspects of the "disastrous" outcomes of these policies. A report published by the World Bank in 2007 on the assessment of poverty in Egypt drew attention to the

---

14 For more details see *The Egyptian Constitution 1971*, https://www.google.com.eg/url?sa=t&rct=j&q=&esrc=s&source=web&cd=3&ved=0ahUKEwjrtvON_57SAhUQsBQKHTPsBkIQFggvMAI&url=http%3A%2F%2Ffaculty.ksu.edu.sa%2F74394%2FDocuments%2F%25D8%25AF%25D8%25B3%25D8%25AA%25D9%2588%25D8%25B1%25201971%2520PDF.pdf&usg=AFQjCNHoua6AmjiFCduD2vGNGHTpJqPQOQ&sig2=4yC15Bau_uHFywfXsxNqZQ and the amended Article 4 of *The Egyptian Constitution 2007*, http://www.constitutionnet.org/sites/default/files/constitution_of_2007-arabic.pdf

15 Egypt had an even lower rank in 2008: 115 out of 180 countries. For more details, see Transparency International 2007; 2008.

pitfalls of the reforms and their consequences on the increasing rates of poverty. By that time, according to the same report, poverty rates had reached 40%, with the highest concentration in rural Egypt, particularly in Upper Egypt (World Bank 2007:iii–iv). Further, the report indicated that two main areas in the economy were seriously affected by the reforms: the agricultural sector, on the one hand, and the food market, on the other. Similarly, the report showed that there was an increase in cultivated land during the same period, which resulted from the reclamation of new lands in the desert that were allocated to agro-industrial enterprises, but to few young farmers. This meant that the agricultural land in the Nile Valley, which was largely cultivated by small poor-household farmers, did not witness any noticeable growth in productivity during the reform years, and the rural poor remained stranded in a deeper poverty. On the food front, the conditions were no better; the depreciation of the Egyptian pound contributed to the increase in food prices, which in turn had a detrimental effect on poor households, both rural and urban, who allocate a high percentage of their income to food. Finally, according to the report, the outcome of those reforms forced the government to increase its expenditure on food subsidies, something that the World Bank and the government had for years been desperately trying to remove (World Bank 2007:54–55, 57–58, 62).

Several intriguing questions arise from this account. For example, how is it that international organizations such as the World Bank could have two or three different, if not opposing, registers in their analysis of the ERSAP reforms? While the World Bank did recognize at a very early stage the damaging effects of the reforms on the poor, together with the IMF they have engineered the terms of the economic reforms and contributed actively in devising the required policies for their implementation. In its assessment of poverty and the agricultural sector in Egypt, the World Bank acknowledged that the country was in a disastrous situation, and yet it persisted in praising the government for its achievement at the level of the macroeconomy. It even went as far as ranking Egypt as the first country in developing its business environment and in implementing the reforms. While the regime celebrated its achievements and the praises it had earned from the World Bank, other agencies ranked Egypt as a highly corrupt environment, and it was public knowledge at the time that many parliamentary deputies were known as "deputies of services," who were heavily involved in fraud and illegal activities (Blaydes 2011:55–56). These contradictions not only raise the question of how such organizations develop their visions for development and set their criteria to measure achievements and failures, but they also illustrate the complicity between these organizations and authoritarian regimes as well as the ruling elites. Thus it is not surprising that poverty issues and the food crisis, which erupted a year later, were mostly justified as the unintended consequence of the reform recipes and the inefficiencies of the government's performance. As result, these unintended consequences, which the World Bank mentioned, were not viewed as an indication of the regime's failure in implementing the policies, or even as a signal to the dangerous implications they could have for the stability of the regime. To the contrary, the flaws in the policies were seen as reversible issues that only time could redress. Finally, it would be safe to say that both the regime and the international organizations failed to read between the lines to capture, in advance, the sociopolitical consequences of the reforms, which contributed a year later to the food crises and set the scene for the January 2011 uprisings.

In line with their approach to the poor and their vision of economic development in Egypt, the 2008 food crisis was thus seen as a non-political issue that could take a political turn if left unattended. The crisis is represented as an unfortunate coincidence during the implementation of national economic development, which added to the plight of the vulnerable social categories who were to benefit at a later stage of the economic structural adjustment. But at no point during this period did the government or international agencies question the principles and the system upon which ERSAP was being implemented. Only a few emergency measures were adopted to supply food to the masses, such as deploying the military and the police to increase the production and distribution of subsidized bread to the 'hungry.' Moreover, public performances and discourses were produced to appease public opinion by acknowledging the existence of hunger among the poor, and publicizing the fund-raising campaigns among the business community to convey a feeling of social solidarity and cohesion. Against its expectations and agreements with international donors, the government finally had to delay the implementation of measures for the gradual removal of food subsidies until the end of the crisis, which of course never saw the light under the Mubarak regime. Perhaps this crisis and the delays in the removal of food subsidies came as a blessing to the government, for it did not need to confront an already angry population while it was in preparation for the parliamentary elections of 2010 and the presidential ones in 2011.

'Hunger' between Scientific Measurements and 'Palliative' Projects

In general, the FAO assesses the food situation of a country in relation to food security. The more the food conditions of a region deviate from the food-security criteria, the closer they are situated to food insecurity; at the far end of the spectrum of food security and insecurity lies the category of undernourishment. Therefore, hunger is measured in relation to undernourishment, which "refers to the proportion of the population whose dietary energy consumption is less than a pre-determined threshold. This threshold is country specific and is measured in terms of the number of kilocalories required to conduct sedentary or light activities. The undernourished are also referred to as suffering from food deprivation" (FAO 2008:2).[16] This explanation of food security and insecurity corresponds largely to the biological needs of food intake and its impact on human abilities to conduct daily activities. Further, the determinant factors for food security involve the ability of the population to access food both economically and physically in a stable manner over time.

Based on these official criteria and measurements, the international media portrayed Egypt in images that corresponded more to the food-insecurity end of the scale: large numbers of the population queuing endlessly for food, fighting over a loaf of bread, and dying in a sinister way while waiting in front of bakeries. Such scenes were mediatized worldwide, and triggered the concerns of the Egyptian government as well as UN organizations.[17] Jointly they publicized their efforts and campaigns to develop alternative strategies to combat hunger, appease public opinion, and provide bread to the 'hungry' masses. Thus, while the international media were covering the workers' strikes in Mahalla and Mansura and

---

16 According to the FAO (2008:1), four criteria determine food security: 1) physical availability of food; 2) economic and physical access to food; 3) food utilization; 4) stability of the other three dimensions over time.

17 McGreal, "Egypt: Bread Shortages, Hunger and Unrest"; BBC News, "Egypt Court Convicts Food Rioters," December 15, 2008, http://news.bbc.co.uk/2/hi/middle_east/7784091.stm

the ongoing protests, as well as the social feuds and conflicts due to food shortages, the government seems to have been trying to disentangle the association that many intellectuals and activists established between the various claims for democracy, the workers' calls for economic and political rights, and the conflicts around food shortages. By isolating the food crisis from the overall political scene, the government, with the support of the international agencies, was seeking to contain the crisis within the framework of an unfortunate conjuncture related to external factors—the global food crisis—which lay beyond the control of the state.

At this point, 'hunger' became a term that was gradually integrated into the local official press jargon. It referred implicitly to the impact of unexpected and/or quasi-metaphysical factors that hindered the relentless efforts deployed by the state to achieve economic development. In this light, community and charity organizations were heavily solicited to participate in alleviating this national crisis; they received enormous state support through media promotions and public events, and the 'rich' were invited to contribute with their efforts and funds, and become the providers to the poor. Hunger was thus transformed into a non-political issue, and solutions to combat it were to be found in the collective societal endeavors and charity, rather than within state policies. Accordingly, it became a depoliticized concern in the official public discourse, which no longer engaged the state but rendered the partnership between society and its corporate enterprises accountable for success in eradicating hunger.

The Egyptian Food Bank: Agency of Corporate Development, Morality, and Religious Responsibility

In 2010, and in line with UN organizations' objectives, the official newspaper *Al-Ahram* published an editorial on hunger in Egypt, to show how the partnership between the state and corporate organizations was successfully deploying efforts to eradicate hunger by 2025. The editorial starts with the premise that poverty is a reality; governments, states, UN organizations, and NGOs combined cannot eradicate poverty, but societies could still eradicate hunger, which is often related to poverty. In fact, hunger is not the outcome of a poor economic system but the result of a lack of social solidarity, morality, and religion.[18] It is in the context

---

18 Gihan al-Gharabawi, "al-Taʿam likul fam" [Food for Each Mouth], *Al-Ahram*, May 12, 2010, http://www.ahram.org.eg/archive/164/2010/5/12/3/19952/219.aspx

of this approach that the Egyptian Food Bank (EFB) was founded in 2006 by a group of businessmen, aiming at "serving society and helping those in need by specializing in Hunger . . . [EFB was] to be converted into a national project that serves all governorates" (Sukar 2014). The principles and the vision of the bank were developed and elaborated in a book authored by the executive director of the Egyptian Food Bank at the time, entitled "Hunger and Religious, Moral, and Social Responsibility" (Sukar 2014). The book is a reminder to the business community and the rich of their religious and moral obligations toward the poor, and calls upon their sense of civic duty to assist the government and the state at large to combat the ghost of hunger that is hindering the country's socioeconomic development efforts. The book and the vision of EFB both call upon the social responsibility of the business community to create a partnership with the government and the NGOs.[19]

EFB's board of trustees consists of CEOs and CEO deputies, consultants, and directors of major business companies in Egypt who have close relationships with the former ruling National Democratic Party (NDP) and the ruling elite.[20] Its organizational chart indicates that it operates as a corporation based on a hierarchical structure with all the required managerial departments. In addition, the EFB has a series of specialized departments for the identification of projects, their planning, and their implementation. There is a research department, an evaluation and NGO identification department, and departments for the management of NGOs, projects and programs, operations, and quality control.[21] EFB coordinates its activities both regionally and internationally with food banks and international organizations.[22]

---

[19] Nermin Qotb, "Nahw Misr khaliya min al-guʻ ʻam 2025: maʻan did al-guʻ" [Toward an Egypt without Hunger in the Year 2025: Together against Hunger], *Al-Ahram*, September 8, 2008.

[20] Information retrieved on February 27, 2017 from https://www.egyptianfoodbank.com/ar/مجلس-الإدارة

[21] Information retrieved on February 27, 2017 from https://www.egyptianfoodbank.com/ar/الإدارات

[22] For more details about EFB's regional and international activities, see https://www.egyptianfoodbank.com/en/regionally-and-internationally. According to its 2013 budget report, EFB's budget was around LE 106 million: https://www.egyptianfoodbank.com/sites/default/files/PDFs/EFB_Balance_Sheet_2012.pdf

On its website, EFB lists a large variety of activities, including awareness campaigns against food waste, the enhancement of the capabilities of the poor, the organization of charitable works, and the 'feeding' programs for the poor. These programs are interesting to examine in the context of this discussion, because they illustrate EFB's perceptions and practical approaches toward those whom they have identified as "the poor who need to be 'fed.'" The feeding programs have several components, such as the Sacrifice Vouchers (both local and imported), the Vows and Redemption Program, the Monthly Feeding Package Program, the Almsgiving Program, and the Dignified Life Program.[23] Many corporations participate in these programs as donors, as money collectors, and as providers of facilities and equipment. The EFB multiplied its Monthly Feedings packages considerably over eight years; they started with 36,000 families in 2006, reaching 1,200,000 beneficiaries nationwide by 2011.[24]

Perhaps the most important programs were the Vows and Redemption Vouchers and the Sacrifice Vouchers. Because of their religious nature, these programs are usually authorized by the Ministry of Awqaf (Ministry of Endowments) and endorsed by the Dar al-Ifta' (Fatwa Council). The Vows and Redemption Vouchers are payments made by Muslims who wish to make a religious gift on any special occasion in their life course, such as childbirth, the acquisition of a property or valuable commodity, or a lifesaving event. Many Muslims perform this ritual, which is dedicated to God through a gift in the form of a slaughtered animal whose meat is offered to a poor Muslim. Traditionally, the gift was offered directly by the wealthier Muslim to the poor Muslim, but in urban areas and in recent years, the EFB has introduced the idea of procurement, by which the Muslim offering the gift delegates EFB to perform the ritual, and the money is paid through any of its representatives. For example, banks and corporations such as Vodafone Cash Call and Facebook collect the money and issue the voucher to the donor.[25]

---

23 For details, see https://www.egyptianfoodbank.com/en

24 Heba Ragab, "al-Masraf al-mutahid 'yatrah sak al-'adhiya bi-l-ta'awun ma'a bank al-ta'am" [United Bank of Egypt offers Sacrifice Vouchers in Cooperation with the Egyptian Food Bank], *Garidat al-Mal*, October 4, 2013, http://www.almalnews.com/Pages/StoryDetails.aspx?ID=108368

25 For more details, see https://www.egyptianfoodbank.com/en/program/vows-and-redemptions

EFB addressed a major issue related to the donors of the gift who find it difficult to access a place to slaughter the animal, and to identify the needy poor who would be eligible to receive the gift. EFB thus became the mediator and the negotiator between the donor of the gift and the poor. The Sacrifice Vouchers are based on the same principles as the Vows and Redemptions Vouchers, but they are exclusively dedicated to animal sacrifice during the Bairam. The vouchers are issued according to the market price of the meat per kilogram and its provenance (local or imported meat).[26]

Very quickly, EFB became a sophisticated apparatus that developed a feeding machinery operating around the clock during high seasons, such as Ramadan and Bairam. It is managed as a corporate institution with all the accompanying managerial equipment and staff. It coordinates its activities with other corporate institutions and signs agreements accordingly. For example, the CEO of the United Bank in Egypt, established in 2006, who works in close coordination with the EFB Slaughtering Voucher program, declared in an interview that "with the continuous success of the Sacrifice Voucher, a joint product developed with EFB, the bank was able to institutionalize a modern and civilized product that respects religious rituals, minimizes waste in the slaughtering operation, and addresses effectively the problem of hunger. For example, the remains of meat cuts are processed with vegetables, canned, and distributed to poor families."[27] In the world of business and development, the EFD would have scored high on the "best practices" and "success stories" scales.

The Hungry and the 'Eater'

It is in the context of the corporate and development worlds that the term 'hunger' has been given specific meanings by the principal actors in this story: government agencies and the corporate sector. They presented hunger as the product of an invisible hand that works unintentionally against the state's efforts for development, the well-being of the population, and its future prosperity. They also represented the food crisis as an unintended consequence of unexpected global circumstances, which

---

26 Details were retrieved on February 19, 2015 from https://www.egyptianfoodbank.com/en/sacrifice-deed
27 Ragab, "al-Masraf al-mutahid."

should be addressed in a depoliticized manner. Practical solutions were to be found, and pragmatic actions were to be driven by moral and religious engagements, based on the efficient system of corporate management.

In fact, at no point during this crisis was there a serious examination of the reasons behind the acute social inequalities the regime has produced over the years. For decades, and especially since the implementation of ERSAP, the government and the development agencies viewed scarcity, poverty, and food deprivation as a normal and unfortunate outcome of modernization that only time and the efforts of social responsibility could heal. For them, the hungry are the masses who have no names or voices; they are numbers and figures, as presented in the EFB reports. And most important, the 'hungry' need to be 'fed' in a quantifiable and measurable manner in order for them to fulfill their biological functions and assume their role in society. Thus, with the retreat of the state from welfare policies, religious, corporate, and civic responsibilities were called upon to fulfill part of this task and help in feeding the deprived masses. The approach to the 2008 food crisis was thought to be comprehensive, for in many ways, it satisfied the main players. For the ordinary Muslim who observes religious rituals, making donations to EFB would allow him to fulfill comfortably his religious obligations. For the corporations, working closely with the EFB would give them credibility on the social responsibility scale, media coverage, and financial gains through their business cooperation with EFB. The main players thus benefit on all fronts, but although the main subjects of this story are being fed, they remain unknown, unheard, and reduced to a perpetual state of scarcity.

As Escobar suggests, "What makes economics possible is a perpetual situation of scarcity; the existence of a humanity that labors under the threat of death. There is still scarcity only to the extent that people represent to themselves things they do not have" (Escobar 2005:152, 170).

Policy makers recognized hunger as a reality in Egypt, and researchers accepted that food deprivation is reflected in levels of calorie consumption and accessibility to food, and thus they were both able to mediatize it as a semi-chronic condition of an emerging capitalist nation, which suffers from scarcity of needed resources. It is in this context that experts and policy makers represented food scarcity to themselves and to the majority of the population: things we don't have and for which society must create a solidarity system to help the vulnerable to survive. It is no surprise, therefore, to find that the core of the official discourse that addressed the food crisis was based on corporate, moral, and religious ideologies. But, as Escobar argues, this leaves little room for us to grasp the reality of the world, and, I would add, the reality of the persistence of food deprivation in the finitude of economic resources (Escobar 2005:152, 170). Social morality, duties, and obligations are powerful terms that were to justify to the 'masses' the unfortunate outcomes of the economic reforms, but this ideology failed to save the regime from the revolts of the same population they addressed, three years later.

In conclusion, the concept of hunger should be understood not in relation to the 'feeding' solution of a hungry population, but as a crisis that needs to be directly linked to and situated within the ongoing sociopolitical struggles and problematized within the dominant sociopolitical system. Further, policy makers and 'experts' seem to forget that behind hunger and the hungry lies 'the eater,' who performs the act of eating: an act that lies beyond the fulfillment of biological functions. This is an 'eater' who taps into the social and cultural meanings of eating, and whose voice has been deliberately omitted and silenced throughout the 2008–2010 period. The eater was reduced to a passive recipient of food whose only concern was to be fed on regular basis.

This is how the government, the corporate institutions, and the world of development saw the hungry at the time, and this is most likely why they failed to see what the future was hiding. Perhaps this reflection would lead us to ask a simple question: who is the 'eater'? Who is this actor and how could we locate him/her within the sociopolitical scene (Fischler 2013). Finally, we could push the reflection further and ask: how do eaters relate to what they eat and why? As Fischler suggests: "We must know what we eat for fear of no longer knowing who we are" (Fischler 2013).

Surely, these questions beg for a larger study that lies beyond the limitations of this chapter.

References

Blaydes, Lisa. 2011. *Elections and Distributive Politics in Mubarak's Egypt*. Cambridge, UK: Cambridge University Press.

Breisinger, Clemens, Perrihan Al-Riffai, Olivier Excker, Risham Abuismail, Jane Waite, and Noura Abdelwehab. 2013. *Tackling Egypt's*

Rising Food Insecurity in a Time of Transition. Joint IFPRI-WFP Country Policy Note, May. http://www.ifpri.org/sites/default/files/publications/ifpriwfppn_egypt.pdf

Escobar, Arturo. 2005. "Economics and the Space of Modernity," *Cultural Studies*, 19(2): 139–75.

FAO (Food and Agricultural Organization). 2008. "An Introduction to the Basic Concepts of Food Security." *Food Security Information for Action, Practical Guides.* http://www.fao.org/docrep/013/al936e/al936e00.pdf

Fischler, Claude. 2013. "Manger: qu'est-ce que cela veut dire?" *Sciences Humaines*, 251, "L'ère culinaire: 15 questions sur l'alimentation" (July–August 2013). Retrieved on August 1, 2013, from: https://www.scienceshumaines.com/manger-qu-est-ce-que-cela-veut-dire_fr_30977.html

IDSC (Egyptian Cabinet Information and Decision Support Center). 2013. *The Cost of Hunger.* http://documents.wfp.org/stellent/groups/public/documents/ena/wfp257981.pdf

Mauss, Marcel. 1980. *Sociologie et Anthropologie.* Paris: PUF.

OECD-FAO. 2008. *Agricultural Outlook 2008–2017.* OECD/FAO 2008:2. http://www.oecd.org/trade/agricultural-trade/40715381.pdf

Sufyan, Alissa. 2007. *The Political Economy of Reform in Egypt: Understanding the Role of Institutions.* Carnegie Papers 5. Washington DC: Carnegie Middle East Center.

Sukar, Reda. 2014. *al-Gu' wa-l-mas'uliya al-diniya wa-l-akhlaqiya wa-l-'igtima'iya* [Hunger and Religious, Moral, and Social Responsibility]. Cairo: Dar al-Fikr al-Arabi.

Transparency International. 2007. "Corruption Perceptions Index 2007." http://www.transparency.org/research/cpi/cpi_2007

Transparency International. 2008. "Corruption Perceptions Index 2008." http://www.transparency.org/research/cpi/cpi_2008

World Bank. 2007. *Arab Republic of Egypt Poverty Assessment Update.* Vol. 1, *Main Report.* https://openknowledge.worldbank.org/bitstream/handle/10986/7642/398850v101OFFI10Update10Main0Report.pdf?sequence=1

CHAPTER 8

Gulf Land Acquisitions in Egypt and Sudan: Food Security or the Agro-commodity Supply Chain?

Christian Henderson

This chapter argues that over the last two decades a food-security discourse has emerged in the Middle East that has been sponsored and supported by the Gulf states. This manifests itself in the form of academic research and policy studies claiming to show that the Gulf states suffer greater food insecurity than other parts of the Arab region. Moreover, the rhetoric of food security is deployed in the acquisition of agricultural land by Gulf investors in Egypt and Sudan. These investments are sometimes portrayed as a 'win-win' situation that can benefit both the host country and the investor. However, evidence suggests that rather than being concerned with addressing the food security of Egypt, Sudan, or the Gulf states, these projects primarily represent a land base for commodities used by regional agro-industrial conglomerates owned by Gulf capital. The crops that are grown on these projects are used for the production of what can be described as "high-value, low nutrition foodstuffs" (Ayeb and Bush 2014), and their distribution is determined by the free market, rather than on the basis of ensuring universal food security. This chapter is based on interviews that were undertaken in Egypt in 2013.

A Food-Security Discourse

According to the 1996 World Food Summit, "Food security, at the individual, household, national, regional and global levels, [is achieved] when all people, at all times, have physical and economic access to sufficient, safe and nutritious food to meet their dietary needs and food preferences for an active and healthy life" (FAO 2003). An earlier definition of the concept also included the importance of insulating the supply of food prices from fluctuations in the market. A statement of the 1974 World Food Summit defined food security as "availability at all times of adequate world food supplies of basic foodstuffs to sustain a steady expansion of food consumption and to offset fluctuations in production and prices" (FAO 2003).

Over the last decade, food security in the Middle East has been the subject of a number of academic studies and policy reports (Woertz 2013; Bailey and Willoughby 2013; Harrigan 2014; Elhadj 2005). These works have brought attention to the food insecurity of the Arab states, but they have tended to blur the inequality in food security that exists within the Arab region and the manner in which the inter-regional trade of crops and commodities can exacerbate this difference. For example, Harrigan treats the region as a whole but does not investigate the inequality that exists between Arab states. Other studies focus specifically on the Gulf states and create an impression that their food insecurity is the most acute in the region. For example, Woertz's book is entitled *Oil for Food: The Global Food Crisis and the Middle East*, suggesting that it examines the whole region, but the majority of his study focuses on the food insecurity of the Gulf states. Other writers, such as Elhadj, promote the Gulf states' policy of food imports based on the theory of comparative advantage, which reinforces the policy of importing food in order to ensure food security.

Some of these studies have been sponsored by the Gulf states, whose considerable financial resources have allowed them to fund conferences, governance institutions, and research that address their food-security needs—including in universities and think tanks in the west. In 2013 Chatham House, a think tank for international affairs in London, published a report entitled "Edible Oil: Food Security in the Gulf" (Bailey and Willoughby 2013) which was funded by the court of the crown prince of Abu Dhabi, Mohamed bin Zayed al-Nahyan. In 2010 the Economist Intelligence Unit published a report called "The GCC in 2020: Resources for the Future" which included a chapter on food security (EIU 2010). The report was sponsored by the Qatar Financial Centre Authority, a government institution.

The Gulf states themselves have also established think tanks to address this problem. For example, Qatar founded the National Food Security

A Food-Security Discourse

Programme in 2008 and the Global Dry Land Alliance (GDLA) in 2010. The GDLA's members include all Gulf states, a number of other Arab states, and several non-Arab states, such as Kazakhstan, Mexico, and South Africa. One of the organization's aims is to "facilitate the cooperative participation of its members in international and multilateral food security related efforts" (GDLA 2015). In 2010, the UAE established the Food Security Centre with the aim of improving the country's food security. Abu Dhabi has also hosted food-security conferences; in 2014 it sponsored the World Food Security Summit, which featured as speakers several government officials and managers of food and commodity companies in the Gulf. The conference featured sessions on the potential for trade and investment to improve food security. In another example, Saudi Arabia established the King Abdullah Initiative for Saudi Agricultural Investment Abroad with a capital of US $800 million in 2010. The institution is tasked with providing interest-free loans to Saudi companies that are considering agricultural investments outside of Saudi Arabia.[1]

The prescription of much of this discourse is to recommend the import of agricultural commodities from abroad and the phasing out of domestic horticulture due to its intense use of the Gulf's dwindling water reserves. As will be discussed below, this has involved the establishment of offshore agricultural projects in countries such as Egypt and Sudan as well as many other locations in the global South. In the critical literature, these acquisitions have been called land grabs; they are considered to infringe on land tenure rights in the host states and have often been allocated land with considerable water resources.

Despite the attention that has been given to the food security of the Gulf states, they are probably more food-secure than many other countries in the Arab region. According to one study, the UAE, Kuwait, and Saudi Arabia have the most affordable food in the Middle East and North Africa after Israel. In terms of affordability these three states score above 80, while Egypt scores just 55 (EIU 2015). Moreover, there has been an increase in the rate of malnutrition in Egypt, and the country's poor are estimated to spend as much as 50 percent of their income

---

[1] I. Elliot, "Interview: Dr. Saad A. Khalil Esa, King Abdullah Initiative for Agricultural Investment Abroad," *Saudi Arabia News*, March 13, 2014, https://oryxsa.com/2014/03/13/interview-dr-saad-a-khalil-esa-king-abdullah-initiative-for-agricultural-investment-abroad/.

on food. Sudan also suffers from food insecurity and there have been reports of famine in certain regions of the country, such as Darfur.

Land Investments in Egypt and Sudan
Over the last two decades, Gulf investors have made a number of large-scale acquisitions of land in Egypt and Sudan. These investments have mostly taken place in the 'New Lands,' that is, land that has been reclaimed from the desert, irrigated, and prepared for agricultural use. The projects involve thousands of acres, often in remote areas far from the main urban centers. Gulf capital, more than any other foreign capital, played a central role in these projects, some of which were launched under the direct control of powerful branches of the state such as the military and the presidency. As a result, the plans received considerable support from the host state. In the case of Egypt, the government often provides infrastructure such as phone lines, roads, and water pipes (Lang 2001:185). These projects have also benefited from subsidized diesel fuel and fertilizer, and they are often exempt from taxes for the first 10 or 20 years.

In a well-known example, Prince Al-Waleed bin Talal al-Saud, a wealthy businessman and a member of the Saudi ruling family, was a cornerstone investor in Toshka, a large project in southern Egypt that was launched in the mid 1990s. Toshka was an ambitious project. The initial plans featured proposals for housing, industry, and vast areas of agricultural land. The project is 660,000 feddans (267,000 hectares) in size, and was granted the use of up to 10 percent of Egypt's total allocation of Nile River water (Milliman and Farnsworth 2011:147). Al-Waleed was initially granted a holding that was 100,000 feddans (40,500 hectares) in size at the time of purchase in 1998, a tract that has since been reduced considerably following a legal case in 2011.[2] In an example of how the state subsidized foreign investors, the land was sold at a price that was far below the market rate: Al-Waleed's Kingdom Agriculture Development Company (KADCO) paid around US \$6 per feddan.[3] At this price, an Egyptian smallholder paid more for a

---

[2] "Egypt Freezes Saudi Prince Alwaleed Land," Reuters, April 10, 2011, http://www.reuters.com/article/us-egypt-alwaleed-idUSTRE7392GT20110410.

[3] "Egyptian Government and Saudi Prince Reach Agreement on Toshka," *al-Ahram Online*, April 20, 2011, http://english.ahram.org.eg/NewsContent/3/12/10457/Business/Economy/Egyptian-government-and-Saudi-prince-reach-agreeme.aspx.

feddan of land than a Saudi billionaire during this period. Other GCC companies continue to control more than half of the land on the project; currently, four Gulf investors own or rent 327,634 feddans (132,588 hectares).[4] Other investors in the project include the al-Rajhi family and al-Dahra, a company owned by the UAE government.

Elsewhere in Egypt, Gulf companies are the largest foreign investors in the Sharq al-Oweinat project, and four Gulf-owned firms rent or own 157,284 feddans (63,650 hectares) of land on a project totaling 267,000 feddans (108,051 hectares).[5] Irrigation for the project has been undertaken through the drilling of boreholes into the Nubian Sandstone Aquifer System, one of the largest aquifers in the world.[6] Given its size, this aquifer could be of great importance to Egypt in terms of food security and as a water reserve, although it is considered to be nonrenewable, as the aquifer does not recharge.

In addition to these state-led projects, private Gulf companies have also established their own farms on land reclaimed from the desert. In one example, the Saudi food conglomerate Savola has recently established a farm in Abu Qurqas in Minya Governorate. The company has sought permission from the government to reclaim up to 100,000 feddans (40,468 hectares) irrigated with groundwater.[7]

In Sudan, Gulf-owned companies have also been involved with similar projects. In 2013 a Saudi company announced that it was investing $800 million in a farm in Sudan that by 2019 would export around 750,000 tons a year of livestock feed to Saudi Arabia.[8] The UAE-owned company Jenaan has a joint venture with the Sudanese government called Amtaar involving 137,000 feddans (55,441 hectares) of reclaimed

---

4 These figures were compiled from a variety of sources, including media articles and company websites.

5 These figures were also compiled from a variety of sources, including media articles and company websites.

6 The aquifer stretches across Chad, Libya, Egypt, and Sudan and is estimated to contain 150,000 km^3 of water (Ibrahim and Ibrahim 2003:47).

7 "18 Sharika wa mustathmer yataqadamun bi-talabat li-takhsis aradi bi-mashro' 1.5 milyoun feddan," Arab Yanoo, February 2, 2016, http://arabyanoo.com/23886#.WJRjcnVSuko.

8 U. Laessing, "Lebanese Farmland Firm to Invest up to $800 Million in Sudan," Reuters, May 21, 2013, http://www.reuters.com/article/sudan-lebanon-food-idUSL6N0E 21Y720130521.

land. A project by a company called Agrogate, which may include Gulf investors, is involved the construction of a new road between Egypt and Sudan and the development of two million feddans (809,371 hectares) of agricultural land as well as a free zone and mining operations.[9] As of the time of writing, this project has not broken ground. In another example, one interviewee pointed to a case where a farm in Sudan was being offered to a Saudi investor with water rights of around 5 percent of Sudan's total annual allocation of Nile River water.[10]

A food-security rhetoric can be observed in the public-relations efforts of the companies operating these projects. They are often portrayed as being mutually beneficial, allowing a 'win-win' situation which aids both the investor and the host state. In a 2014 media interview the Egyptian manager of al-Dahra said, "We consider ourselves to be strategic partners for the Egyptian government in terms of food security."[11] The companies behind these investments even mobilize religion in order to create the appearance of benevolence. An advertisement which described the process of land reclamation in Savola's project in Minya Governorate was preceded by a verse from the Quran which described the importance of the greening of the desert: "And a sign to them is the dead earth: We give life to it and bring forth from it grain so they eat of it" (Al Shoura 2015). Jenaan's Amtaar project in Sudan was described in a media article as aiming to "become a vital organization in world food security, particularly in the Arab world where dry climates and barren lands make it increasingly difficult to feed the fast growing population" (Worldfolio 2015).

One interesting feature of the public-relations campaigns of these companies is the funding of films which feature interviews with company managers and a description of their operations.[12] The films attempt to create the impression that these projects are beneficial for everyone involved. The managers of Jenaan's project in Sudan describe their work with the local people and their gift of a water fountain for the livestock

---

9   K. Abdelaziz, "Egypt, Sudan Plan Joint Farming, Livestock Projects," Reuters, April 5, 2013, http://in.reuters.com/article/sudan-egypt-farming-idINL5N0CS3I220130405.

10 Interview, London, January 25, 2013.

11 M. El Dahan and M. Fick, "UAE–Egypt Alliance Expands to Desert Wheat Venture," Reuters, December 5, 2014, http://www.reuters.com/article/egypt-emirates-wheat-idUSL6N0TP1MA20141205.

12 These films can be found on YouTube.

in the area of their farm. In one interview a manager of the company implies that their project has positive benefits for the environment. However, the management also makes it clear that their business is primarily concerned with making money and with the food security of the Gulf states (Jenaan Investment 2015). The films offer a valuable insight into the operations of these farms, which are often inaccessible due to their remote location and therefore difficult to evaluate.

These schemes are highly water-intensive. Ultimately they prioritize the water needs of agribusiness over smallholder agriculture. Meanwhile, the evidence suggests that there is insufficient water for both the reclamation projects and traditional agriculture (Sims 2014:70). The zero-sum nature of water distribution translates to increasing urgency within policy documents about the need for water use in Egypt to be rationalized and economically justified.[13] The framing of water consumption as being prioritized by the extraction of 'value' is an argument that justifies desert reclamation on the basis that it produces high-value exports and has the capital to invest in water-saving technologies. In this context, large-scale land reclamation projects encapsulate the prioritization of agribusiness companies over smallholders.

Food Security or the Agro-commodity Supply Chain?

In light of the scale of these projects and their implications for the management of resources such as soil and water, as well as the food insecurity of the Egyptian and Sudanese populations, it is worthwhile considering who benefits from them. Do they actually serve the food security of Egypt or even the Gulf states? Or does the food-security discourse merely provide a cover for these projects and allow private companies to secure a productive land base for regional agro-commodity supply chains?

Answering the question of whether these investments serve food security is complicated by the lack of transparency that surrounds foreign investment in reclaimed-land projects. The lack of official, accurate information on these projects is exacerbated by the secretive nature of

---

13 The 2009 World Bank report on food security in the Arab region states that "when farmers are encouraged to pay the full cost of water, they voluntarily switch their use of irrigated land from low-value crops such as wheat to higher-value crops such as fruits and vegetables. In addition, they have incentives to invest in water-saving irrigation technologies" (World Bank 2009).

the companies who operate the farms, whose management is reluctant to give specific information on their operations and where their agricultural products go. Moreover, these projects can be inaccessible for a researcher. In the case of Sharq al-Oweinat a permit is required to visit the project. Aside from tight security, the project's remote location also plays a role in obscuring it from public scrutiny.[14]

With a few exceptions, there is scant evidence to suggest that these land acquisitions serve the definition of food security that was given at the beginning of this chapter. On the contrary, information in media stories and company reports, and estimates made by managers of agribusiness companies, suggest that Gulf farms are mostly used to grow inputs such as cattle fodder, potatoes, and sugar beets for agro-industry in Egypt or the Gulf.

In many cases the produce from Gulf-owned reclamation projects is directly exported to the GCC states and does not enter the Egyptian or Sudanese market, therefore making little contribution to the food security of the host states. One crop which exemplifies this export industry is alfalfa, a water-intensive feed for dairy herds as well as other livestock such as horses and camels. Due to the combination of climate and water sources, the Nile Valley is considered to be one of the best locations in the world for the cultivation of alfalfa, and farms can harvest as many as 10 crops a year. As a result, Egypt and Sudan are now one of the main sources for livestock feed crops in the Gulf.

Alfalfa is often grown on reclaimed land, as the crop is used as a substrate that can fertilize the land and prepare the soil for other crops. Many of the large Gulf-owned projects in Egypt and Sudan produce alfalfa and transport the crop back to Gulf markets by road and sea. A film on Jenaan's Amtaar project in Sudan describes its farm as being like a "military operation" in which the swift transport of the crop is crucial. The video shows convoys of trucks waiting at the farm to transport the crop to Port Sudan, where a weekly shipment of the company's crop departs for Port Khalifa in Abu Dhabi.

---

14 Because of its distance from the Nile Valley, one of the largest investors in the project, Jenaan of the UAE, operates a weekly charter flight to Sharq al-Oweinat airport in order to transport workers and technicians to the project. S. Khan, "Abu Dhabi Firm Grows in Egypt," *The National*, August, 13 2009, http://www.thenational.ae/business/abu-dhabi-firm-grows-in-egypt.

The demand for alfalfa is partly driven by the growth of the dairy and meat sectors in the Gulf states. Over the last two decades, companies in the UAE, Saudi Arabia, and Kuwait have established large industrial dairy farms. One firm, Al Marai, has established the largest integrated dairy operation in the world; its seven farms produce a billion liters of milk a year and own a total herd of 135,000 cows (O'Keeffe 2013). Partly as a result of these huge dairy operations, the market for livestock forage in Saudi Arabia is estimated to be 4 million tons a year.[15] Such is the extent of this demand that the Saudi government now requires that 1 kilogram of livestock forage be imported for every liter of milk that is exported.[16] In combination with the removal of the government subsidy on domestically produced crops, this regulation is fueling a demand for the import of livestock feed crops from countries such as Egypt.

Alfalfa cultivation has been a profitable activity in Egypt and Sudan. In 2013 the crop was sold at $300 a ton in the Gulf, with an approximate production cost of $150 per ton.[17] However, alfalfa became a sensitive issue among Egyptian government officials, who felt that the crop did little to serve the national market and that its export represented a drain on Egyptian water resources. As a result, the government introduced a tax on alfalfa of around $50 a ton in 2013. Following the introduction of this export duty, some agribusiness companies expanded into Sudan, a country perceived as having looser regulations, although the poor infrastructure and security situation can cause problems for companies.[18]

In other cases, Gulf conglomerates have vertically integrated reclaimed lands in Egypt and Sudan into their supply chain. One example is Americana, a Kuwaiti agrofood company owned by the Kharafi family, owners of one of the largest multi-sector conglomerates in Kuwait. One of Americana's subsidiaries is Farm Frites, a major

---

15 Laessing, "Lebanese Farmland Firm," 2013.
16 "Saudi Livestock Feed Imports to Reach 2.4 M Tons by 2016," *Arab News*, February 23, 2013, http://www.arabnews.com/corporate-news/saudi-livestock-feed-imports-reach-24-m-tons-2016.
17 Interview, Cairo, September 16, 2013.
18 According to a manager of an agribusiness farm: "The cost of production in Sudan is much cheaper. But there are two problems: roads and security. If you put something on a truck in Sudan you don't know if you will see it again. The road and transport sector in Egypt is much better. You have trains, roads, and even planes."

producer of frozen french fries. Fifty percent of Farm Frites' potato supply is grown on reclaimed land in Egypt (Americana Group 2012). Much of this crop is destined for Gulf markets: Farm Frites has 35 percent of the Kuwaiti and Emirati markets, 14 percent of the Saudi market, 45 percent of the Bahraini market, and 42 percent of the Qatari market (Americana Group 2012). Besides being purchased by individual consumers, Farm Frites products are also likely to be used by Americana's chains of fast-food restaurants, of which there are 1,550 across the Middle East.

Another example of land in Egypt and Sudan being vertically integrated into agro-industry is the sugar industry. Savola, which is a Saudi agrofood conglomerate, owns United Sugar Company, which has up to 70 percent of the market for sugar in Saudi Arabia, part of which it serves from its factory in Egypt (Savola Foods 2015). In order to meet demand for its factory, in 2014 another Savola company, the Alexandria United Company for Land Reclamation, launched a land reclamation project near Abu Qurqas in the Minya Governorate to grow sugar beets. Another company that has vertically integrated reclaimed land is Juhayna, which is partly owned by Saudi investors. Juhayna owns two reclamation companies for cattle feed such as alfalfa, with a total area of 8,000 feddans (3,240 hectares). In some cases, companies that own farms on reclaimed land projects sell to agro-industrial companies. In an interview an employee of KADCO said that he sells alfafa to Danone, the French dairy producer.[19]

The use of reclaimed land projects for these crops is of questionable benefit to food security in Egypt or the Gulf, as the crops are often processed into high-value, low-nutrition products. Moreover, the products of companies such as Americana and Savola are unaffordable for many Egyptians and are only accessible to the middle classes. For example, the milk that is produced by companies such as Juhayna can be almost four times the price of *baladi* ('country') milk that comes from smaller producers.[20]

In a minority of cases, Gulf companies with land in Egypt and Sudan are growing crops which can actually be considered beneficial to food security in the host states. In these cases, the companies have

---

19 Interview, Cairo, November 12, 2013.
20 Interview, Cairo, November 12, 2013.

sought to take advantage of the price offered by the Egyptian government for domestically grown wheat, which tends to be higher than the international price. Between 2013 and 2014 the international price for a ton of wheat was US $300, while the Egyptian government price for domestically grown wheat was US $400. In 2013, UAE-owned Jenaan announced that it was ending its strategy of growing livestock feed on its farms in Egypt in favor of growing wheat.[21] Executives of the company said the export tax on alfalfa was hitting their profit margins, but added that they had been asked by the Abu Dhabi government to assist with "Egypt's food security" and that this was one of the reasons behind the decision to grow wheat. Another UAE company, al-Dahra, claims on its website that it produces 50,000 metric tons of wheat that is destined for the local market, although it does not say whether its client is the Egyptian state (aldahra.com). Regardless, the benefit of these companies' wheat production for sale to the Egyptian government is debatable, given that they are likely to already have received some form of state subsidy in the course of establishing their farm on the reclamation project, in the form of cheap land, subsidized diesel, and a tax break. Hence the receipt of a second subsidy in the form of a higher purchase price represents 'double dipping' and allows these companies to make even larger profits at the expense of the Egyptian state.[22]

Finally, some Gulf companies claim to provide farmers with subsidized or non-market supplies of commodities such as alfalfa. Companies like Jenaan have created an image that they are providing support for smallholders. Their promotional film features an Emirati woman in traditional dress who is a "beneficiary of the fodder support program," although it does not say how much livestock she has. The woman expresses thanks for this support, specially to Mohammed bin Zayed, the crown prince of Abu Dhabi. It is not clear how many small farmers this program actually serves, and in any case the number of farmers in the UAE is small (agriculture is estimated to employ around 4 percent

---

21 M. El Dahan, "Jenaan Changes Egypt Strategy to Wheat for Local Market," Reuters, November 25, 2013, http://www.reuters.com/article/uae-jenaan-egypt-idUSL5N0JA1VL20131125.

22 It is also possible that these companies' concern with the Egyptian wheat supply was behind the UAE's attempt to support President Abd al-Fatah al-Sisi after he came to power in the coup of July 2013.

of the Emirati population). Instead, the company primarily seems to be engaged with making money by directing its products to the market. According to a statement in the film: "First and foremost, the men of Amtaar run a business, a very productive one."

Conclusion

The food-security discourse that is applied in connection with land acquisitions in Egypt and Sudan suggests that these projects can serve universal food security in the host states and in the Gulf. This notion has been buttressed by the emergence of a regional food-security policy discourse which has received considerable funding and support from the Gulf states. This discourse assumes that the Gulf's reliance on imports makes them some of the most vulnerable states in the Arab region, despite evidence that suggests that food insecurity is worse in poorer countries in the region. There is little evidence to show that these land acquisitions are managed with food security as a primary interest; they are chiefly concerned with serving the market. This is indicated by their vertical integration into the supply chains of agro-industry in the Gulf and Egypt and the fact that much of the produce is exported straight to the Gulf.

The cases described in this chapter suggest that the discourse of food security requires scrutiny, especially when it involves the import of food from poorer countries. In the case of the acquisition of land in Egypt and Sudan by Gulf companies, the use of the food-security discourse obfuscates the use of the host government's national resources in order to supply regional agro conglomerates with inputs that are used for high-value, low-nutrition commodities that have a questionable ability to fulfil the definition of food security.

References

Americana Group. 2012. *Americana Annual Report*. http://www.americana-group.net/portal/PDF/investor_relations/annual_report_2012.pdf.

Ayeb, H., and R. Bush. 2014. "Small Farmer Uprisings and Rural Neglect in Egypt and Tunisia." Middle East Research and InformationProject272.http://www.merip.org/mer/mer272/small-farmer-uprisings-rural-neglect-egypt-tunisia.

References

Bailey, R., and R. Willoughby. 2013. "Edible Oil: Food Security in the Gulf." Energy, Environment and Resources Briefing Paper 2013/03. Chatham House. https://www.chathamhouse.org/sites/files/chathamhouse/public/Research/Energy,%20Environment%20and%20Development/bp1113edibleoil.pdf.

EIU (Economist Intelligence Unit). 2010. "The GCC in 2020: Resources for the Future." http://graphics.eiu.com/upload/eb/GCC_in_2020_Resources_WEB.pdf.

———. 2015. "The Global Food Security Index." http://foodsecurityindex.eiu.com/Index.

Elhadj, E. 2005. "Experiments in Achieving Water and Food Self-sufficiency in the Middle East." Boca Raton (Florida): http://www.dissertation.com/book.php?method=ISBN&book=1581122985

FAO (Food and Agriculture Organization of the United Nations). 2003. "Food Security: Concepts and Measurement." In *Trade Reforms and Food Security: Conceptualizing the Linkages*, ch. 2. http://www.fao.org/docrep/005/y4671e/y4671e06.htm.

GDLA (Global Dry Land Alliance). 2015. "Vision and Mission." http://globaldrylandalliance.com/en-us/about/visionmission.aspx.

Harrigan, J. 2014. *The Political Economy of Arab Food Sovereignty*. Basingstoke: Palgrave Macmillan.

Ibrahim, F., and B. Ibrahim. 2003. *Egypt: An Economic Geography*. London: I.B. Tauris.

Jenaan Investment. 2015. "Jenaan Investment." YouTube. https://www.youtube.com/watch?v=fhHZebLCJLY.

Lang, J. 2001. *Notes of a Potato Watcher*. College Station: Texas A&M University Press.

Milliman, J., and K. Farnsworth. 2011. *River Discharge to the Coastal Ocean*. Cambridge, UK: Cambridge University Press.

O'Keeffe, P. 2013. "How Almarai Produces 1 Billion Litres of Milk from 75,000 Dairy Cows in the Saudi Arabian Desert." *Irish Farmers Journal*, November 7. http://www.farmersjournal.ie/how-almarai-produces-1-billion-litres-of-milk-from-75-000-dairy-cows-in-the-saudi-arabian-desert-148989/.

Savola Foods. 2015. "Savola." http://Savolafoods-eg.com.

Al Shoura, Mohamed. 2015. "Savola AUCR, Magmou'at Savola." YouTube. https://www.youtube.com/watch?v=RxyCkUoGWQM.
Sims, D. 2014. *Egypt's Desert Dreams: Development or Disaster?* Cairo: American University in Cairo Press.
Woertz, E. 2013. *Oil for Food: The Global Food Crisis and the Middle East.* Oxford: Oxford University Press.
World Bank. 2009. "Improving Food Security in Arab Countries." Washington: World Bank. http://siteresources.worldbank.org/INTMENA/Resources/FoodSecfinal.pdf.
Worldfolio. 2015. "An Agricultural Revolution by Amtaar Investment." http://www.theworldfolio.com/news/an-agricultural-revolution-by-amtaar-investment/3733/.

CHAPTER 9

Politics of Food Aid: From Politicization to Integration

Khaled Mansour

At the beginning of the [1990s] ... aid agencies tried to recruit states for their cause, by the beginning of the next decade they had discovered that states had already co-opted humanitarianism for their interests.
(Barnett 2011:172)

Introduction

Several years before Barnett published *Empire of Humanity: A History of Humanitarianism* in 2011, it became painfully clear to many aid workers that humanitarian action had become more deeply and widely politicized over the previous ten years. This was painful, because it made humanitarian workers a direct target of attacks instead of only collateral damage caused by fighting among other parties. A terrorist attack on August 19, 2003 against the UN offices in Baghdad killed 22 people and injured nearly 150.[1] The building housed the UN political delegation, led by a special representative of the secretary general, and the large team of the World Food Programme (WFP), whose main task was to bring in half a million tons of food a month to maintain the country's subsidized food distribution system after the US war dismantled Saddam Hussein's regime. Two months later, another car bomb hit the Baghdad office of the International Committee of the Red Cross, killing at least ten people and injuring many others.

These two bombings were the most spectacular and direct attacks on the UN and the ICRC up until that time, with the largest loss of lives ever

---

1 I worked for the UN World Food Program in Baghdad at the time and survived the attack.

suffered in one single politically motivated incident for either of the two organizations. There was criticism by independent investigators, as well as by the UN staff association, pointing out security lapses. But the politicization of humanitarian aid and the increasing proximity, or more precisely the increasing integration, of the two realms—the political and humanitarian realms of the UN as well as politicization of international humanitarian nongovernmental organizations—might have played a more important role than security gaps in causing these tragic attacks. The Iraq bombings were followed over the next 13 years by more numerous and bloodier attacks against aid workers or installations in Afghanistan, Pakistan, the DRC, Sudan, South Sudan, Somalia, Iraq, Yemen, and finally Syria.[2]

Still, the deteriorating security of aid workers is but a secondary (and probably unintended) consequence of the politicization of humanitarian aid. This politicization or instrumentalization became evident in the civil wars in the Balkans and Kosovo and in Rwanda's genocide in the 1990s, became institutionalized in Afghanistan in 2001, and then moved to deeper levels of integration in 2002 in the months of preparation for the US-led invasion of Iraq. This politicization is now par for the course in Syria (2012–2016), where the aid industry is addressing probably one of its most complex challenges and largest operations ever.[3] By instrumentalization (for political and other purposes), I mean that humanitarian action becomes engaged with multiple other actors (political, economic, military, etc.) to ensure funding, access, and institutional interests at the expense of the three most fundamental humanitarian principles: impartiality,

---

2 About 3,250 aid workers have been killed, injured, or kidnapped in the period 2004–2015 inclusive. Sometimes they were collateral damage (or recklessly attacked by undiscriminating regular forces), but more often they were intentionally targeted by one or more of the warring parties because their role was suspected of directly or indirectly aiding an opponent. Aid workers no longer enjoyed the protection of their flags as neutral providers of aid on the basis of need and humanity and impartial to the conflict parties. They are now more often seen as political tools in the hands of opponents, such as doctors treating the wounded in militia-controlled territories or food aid agencies working only where it is said to be safe by another opponent. For more details on these attacks, patterns, and numbers, see the Aid Workers Security Database at https://aidworkersecurity.org/incidents/report/summary.

3 UN communication officers in the Middle East and South Asia have long reported to their headquarters on local media and public opinion trends, which became gradually more hostile to, or at least cynical about, the UN. I contributed to some of this reporting from Afghanistan, Pakistan, Iraq, Jordan, Egypt, Sudan, and Lebanon when I was a communication adviser for UN humanitarian and peacekeeping operations.

Introduction

neutrality, and independence. Over the past 25 years, humanitarian actors have indeed been increasingly working more closely with political and military institutions on operational, tactical, and strategic levels.

The global liberal peace project that began in the early 1990s after the end of the Cold War and the collapse of the former Soviet Union rested on plans for more democratization, more penetration of free-market ideologies, wider respect for human rights, and more coordination in counterterrorism efforts. This global project accelerated and deepened the politicization of humanitarian aid. Corrupt and crumbling postcolonial states in Africa, Asia, and Latin America, with their kleptocratic security agencies and ruling socioeconomic elites, also helped shape the post-1990 humanitarian space.

Food aid, which is the focus of this chapter, has saved millions of lives since the late nineteenth century, but despite this great achievement and the best intentions of some in the aid community—donors, humanitarian agencies, and recipient governments or authorities—this undertaking is not (and probably could never have been) divorced from politics. Humanitarian organizations and aid workers operate in a hyper-political environment, where power relations are themselves contested in bloody conflicts or disrupted in the aftermath of natural disasters. After water, food is the priced commodity that is most indispensable for survival, but in the case of conflicts it has long served as a weapon to gain an edge over and pressure one's opponents. Aid agencies have long engaged in politics to raise funds, enable operations, and ensure safe access to the people who are meant to receive assistance.

Politicization is not merely the instrumentalization by one party or another of aid agencies, but rather a process in which aid actors also take part. The various actors influence each other. Donors, governments, multilateral aid agencies, NGOs, local communities, militias, and market actors (such as corporations, traders, and farmers) all interact in complex humanitarian crises. A diagram developed by Donini (2012:5) and reproduced in figure 1 depicts the complex network of relations in the realm of humanitarian action. The aid actors have to interact with military, political, market, and civil-society forces with their overlapping and clashing agendas. The original, narrow function of emergency-aid agencies was the saving of lives. Its framework of action has been rooted in international humanitarian law since the late nineteenth century, when Henri Dunant

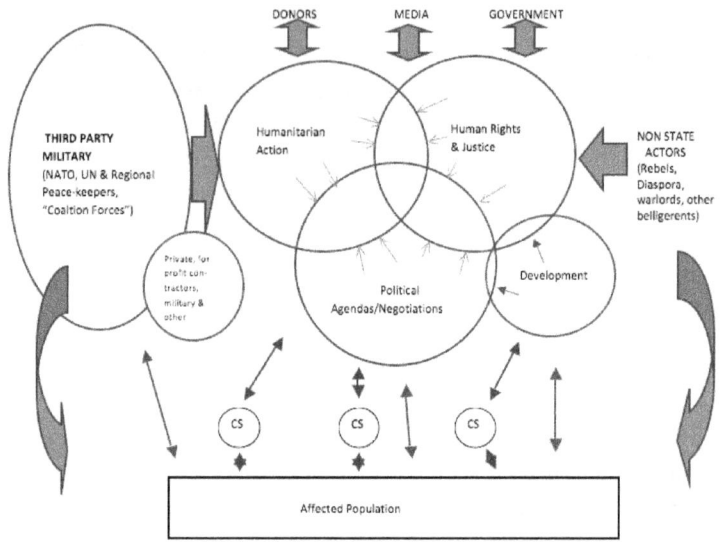

Figure 1. Instrumentalization: actors and agendas

established the International Committee of the Red Cross (ICRC). Now, however, as the diagram shows, emergency aid agencies have to deal with issues related to the root causes of the conflicts: stabilization and medium-term recovery and reconstruction. This means that humanitarian actors have moved from merely working in politically charged circumstances to being part of the political game in many instances.

As they became more bureaucratized and professionalized, aid agencies themselves acquired their own interests, including institutional preservation and growth in a competitive marketplace. Most senior aid managers, with the exceptions of Dunanist organizations like the ICRC or Doctors without Borders, increasingly adopted pragmatic programmatic interventions in conflict situations, a position that often clashed with and undermined the humanitarian principles of impartiality, neutrality, and independence. These compromises become more problematic when they cause suffering to the very people that the humanitarian enterprise is supposed to be helping. In these circumstances, aid agencies can end up not only with mud on their faces but possibly also with blood on their hands. This is what has happened in Somalia, DRC, Sri Lanka, and, as will be shown, is continuing to happen in Syria in 2016.

Introduction

Such overlapping and convergence of political/security concerns and crisis response can be traced as far back as Biafra and Indochina in the 1950s and 1960s. The process of politicization of the humanitarian enterprise accelerated after the end of the Cold War, beginning in 1990, when many western countries shifted away from multilateral modes of interaction in humanitarian assistance to approaches more blatantly subservient to national-security, business, and political interests. Donini, Minear, and Walker (2004) outline various ways in which the political and the humanitarian interact, converge, or overlap. Donini and Walker have even argued that there has never been a "golden age when core humanitarian values took precedence over political or other considerations" (Donini and Walker 2012:244). They outline the structural limitations within the humanitarian enterprise that made the endeavor always politicized in one form or another depending on historical context.

The Iraq bombing in 2003, however, marked a transition from increasing convergence between political and security objectives on the one hand and aid operations on the other hand to an outright integration approach, in which the aid operations become part of the tool box, or "the benevolent side of globalization" (Donini 2012:193). Not only governments but also international aid agencies, NGOs, community organizations, and beneficiaries in conflict areas have political interests and participate in this integration with varying influences—beneficiaries being the weakest in these networks of interdependence.

Multiple pressures are exerted on big aid agencies like the WFP, which operates under political, security, and financial constraints and constrains others in turn. The WFP, however, occupies a prestigious position in a complex network of donors, governments, international NGOs, private-sector suppliers, local civil-society organizations, and other actors in a multi-billion-dollar enterprise. With 15,000 staff members and a budget of US $4.8 billion in 2015, the WFP is the largest aid organization in the world. It assisted 78 million people around the globe in 2015, about 24 percent of whom were in emergency situations in the Middle East (WFP 2016:20).[4] In almost all these Middle East emergencies, major powers such as the US, the UK,

---

4 WFP provided food assistance to Yemen (nine million people), Syria (five million inside the country and two million in neighboring Lebanon and Jordan), Iraq (two million), and Palestine (600,000) (WFP 2016:20).

Russia, and France were implicated in one form or another, including direct bombing, deployment of troops, and arms sales. These are also countries that have permanent seats on the UN Security Council and/ or are among the WFP's largest donors. The US, which is involved in Syria, Afghanistan, and Yemen,[5] provided 40 percent, or two billion dollars, of the WFP's budget in 2015. The UK provided about 10 percent (US $456 million), the European Commission provided 5 percent (US $259 million), and Canada 5.4 percent (US $261 million) (WFP 2016:27).

The US has been no stranger to politicized engagement in international humanitarian aid since Herbert Hoover, who later became the US president, established the American Committee for Relief in Belgium during the First World War and went on to lead relief programs in Poland and the Soviet Union during the famines of 1919–1923. The US was behind the creation of the League of Red Cross Societies, which is now the International Federation of Red Cross and Red Crescent Societies (IFRC), one of the largest humanitarian organizations in the world. The US helped create and still strongly influences leading humanitarian organizations such as UNICEF and the WFP. The fact that UNICEF, for many years, focused on relief and avoided active advocacy for children's rights in sensitive situations, such as the Palestine conflict or international adoption, are but two examples of the remarkable American influence on the organization. The WFP, on the other hand, has distanced itself from the 'right to food' debate, largely due to a strong, Protestant-influenced American preference for philanthropy based on human solidarity rather than on human rights in issues such as basic food needs. The operations of these organizations, as well as American humanitarian NGOs (such as World Vision International, CARE, and the International Rescue Committee), reveal the way in which they are increasingly aligned with US global projects anchored in stability, expanding free markets, democratization, and rule of law. It is no wonder that one secretary of state after

---

5 The US is the largest seller of arms to Saudi Arabia and other members of the coalition fighting in Yemen. The WFP's largest donors are also among the largest arms sellers to countries in the Middle East where the WFP is involved in providing humanitarian aid. See the IHS 2015 report for arms sales at http://news.ihsmarkit. com/press-release/aerospace-defense-security/record-breaking-65-billion-global-defence-trade-2015-fueled

another since the 1990s has described these organizations as "tools" or "force multipliers" in terms of US foreign policy.

The focus on the US does not mean that other major western countries did not adopt a similar manipulative position, especially those with political interests in areas of conflict or the permanent members of the Security Council such as the UK and France. The northern/western roots of the humanitarian aid system (as distinct from 'humanitarianism,' which can be found in many cultures and faiths around the world) are still very evident and can be seen in the preponderance of western senior managers and leaders in large aid organizations.

This broad framework will guide the rest of the chapter, which analyzes the humanitarian operations in Syria (2014–2016) and in Iraq (2002–2003).[6]

The Syria Case

For many years, food assistance has been by far the largest component of any emergency aid operation. This has certainly been the case in Syria, where a civil uprising was exacerbated by the reactions of the ruling regime into a civil war in late 2011 and early 2012. This escalation quickly made the country the theater for a large humanitarian disaster in the same league as Bosnia and Rwanda in the 1990s or Darfur in the mid 2000s. By mid 2016, at least 250,000 Syrians had been killed and over one million injured; one of every two Syrians had to leave home (about 4.8 million left the country altogether, while another 6.5 million were internally displaced). The country's educational and health infrastructure has been decimated.[7]

The total funding for humanitarian action in Syria in the four years from 2012 to 2015 totaled US $6.8 billion. In 2015 alone it was US

---

6 In addition to relying on publicly available resources, I was the WFP spokesperson in Jordan and Iraq for most of 2003 and have intimate knowledge of the operation there. For the Syria case, I spoke with several UN and NGO workers who run the operation in Syria or from Turkey, including during a visit in April 2016 to the Turkish border area of Gaziantep, where cross-border operations are organized. However, I use no confidential information or documents I had access to during my work for the purpose of this study.

7 For an overview of the most credible, and rather conservative, figures for the destructive impact of the civil war in Syria, see OCHA's report at http://www.unocha.org/syrian-arab-republic/syria-country-profile/about-crisis.

$2.4 billion, or 11.7 percent of the global humanitarian expenditure. About 64 percent of the humanitarian funding for Syria in 2015 came from the US and the UK combined. A third of the 2015 funds went to food assistance, more than half of which, about US $442 million, went to the WFP. The WFP alone received nearly 19 percent of all funding that went to Syria's humanitarian operations in 2015.[8]

The untold humanitarian suffering of people in Syria is not merely a byproduct of the civil war, but part and parcel of the war effort itself. Targeting civilians and their basic educational, health, and road infrastructure has been used as a war tactic, largely by the government, but also by the opposing militias. Starvation, denial of medical and other basic humanitarian supplies, destruction of schools and hospitals, and killing of medical staff have all become regular weapons in conducting the war in Syria.[9]

On the ground, aid agencies like the WFP have come under intense political pressure from the government of Bashar al-Assad, which controls most of the Syrian territory, and to a lesser extent from the armed factions. Pressure was also exerted by the main donors and permanent members of the Security Council, who have complex agendas in Syria. The Office for the Coordination of Humanitarian Affairs (OCHA) of the UN, in an evaluation in late 2015, summarized these multiple pressures.

> *With Syria still maintaining its seat at the United Nations, and backed by Russia and China, UN agencies did not consider it possible that they could violate sovereignty. On the other side of this equation, the other three permanent members of the Security Council—France, the US and the UK—were openly backing the opposition to Assad and covertly financing aid across the borders into opposition areas. With the US, the UK and the EU accounting for over half of the official aid flows into the UN humanitarian system, the political pressures were intense.* (Sida, Trombetta, and Panero 2016:11)

---

[8] For details on humanitarian funding, donors, recipients, and programs, see OCHA Financial Tracking Services at https://ftsbeta.unocha.org/countries/206/summary/2015.

[9] For general description and analysis, see reports issued by the OCHA, the ICRC, HRW, and Syrian NGOs such as the Violations Documentation Center and the Syrian Observatory for Human Rights.

The Syria Case

This evaluation concluded that "UN agencies were simply not willing to jeopardize their operations in Syria by taking a tougher stance with the Government . . . [a position that] will surely be scrutinized unfavorably at a later point." Even after the Security Council decided to allow cross-border operation in July 2014, "Damascus-based UN humanitarian agencies have been slow to take advantage of . . . Resolution 2165, and throughout they have been protective of their relationship" with the government of Syria (Sida, Trombetta, and Panero 2016:15).

In Syria, the WFP claimed that through working with the Arab Red Crescent (SARC), which is largely controlled by the government in Damascus, it had distributed food to more than four million people inside Syria every month in 2015. But how much of that aid furthered government interests? Who received aid and who could not? How was this selective operation conducted? In general, most of the food aid in the period 2012–2016 has disproportionately gone into government-controlled areas, while opposition-held areas were largely denied aid and some of them were tightly besieged. The conditions in these besieged areas marginally improved in late 2014, but the partiality of the aid operation persisted.

The most disturbing conditions, including reported starvation to death, existed in besieged and hard-to-reach areas, where 4.6 million people live. As of mid 2016, about 590,000 lived in 18 UN-designated besieged locations, of whom

- nearly 450,000 people were besieged by the government, mainly in rural Damascus;
- about 10,000 were besieged by the government and allied militias in Damascus;
- some 110,000 people in government-controlled parts of Deir al-Zour City were besieged by Islamic State or ISIS;
- some 20,000 people were besieged by armed opposition groups and the Nusrah Front in Fuaa and Kafraya, in Idlib province (UN Secretary General 2016:9).

In April 2016, 88 percent of food aid delivered from inside Syria went into government-controlled areas, while 12 percent went into territories outside its control. Some months provide an "even starker illustration of the government's use of UN aid to further its own agenda." In August 2015, the government directed over 99 percent of UN aid from inside the country to its territories. In 2015, less than 1 percent of people in besieged areas received UN food assistance each month (Syria Campaign 2016:4).

Food assistance reached only 8.7 percent of the people in the besieged, hard-to-reach, and priority cross-line areas[10] in May 2016 (UN Secretary General 2016:9). These numbers jump dramatically up and down from one month to another but they are generally low. Moreover, NGOs and the UN differ on their definitions of what constitutes a besieged area and how many people are in them. While the monthly reports by the UN secretary general put the number of besieged areas at 18, some NGOs make it as high as 46, and while the secretary general's report estimates about 590,000 people in besieged areas, the NGOs raise that number to one million. All the areas unacknowledged by the UN lie in Homs and rural Damascus provinces and are surrounded by the Syrian regime's military and its allied militia (Syria Institute and PAX 2016:9).

NGOs admit the relative improvement of humanitarian access to besieged areas in early 2016, but claim that aid deliveries to non–government controlled areas were "inconsistent, insufficient, and unbalanced due to continuing access restrictions, limiting their effectiveness. Even in communities like Moadamiya and Madaya, which received multiple aid deliveries during the reporting period, siege-related deaths continued to be reported" (Syria Institute and PAX 2016:9).

Part of the noticeable improvement after February 2016 was attributed to the decision of the International Syria Support Group (ISSG) to air-drop food aid in besieged areas. However, the implementation of that decision was severely unbalanced. Western parts of Deir al-Zour, which is government-controlled but surrounded by ISIS troops, stood out "as the only besieged area that has experienced a significant improvement in humanitarian conditions as a result of international efforts shepherded by the ISSG," with as many as 50 drops by the WFP. Other besieged areas did not receive the same treatment, prompting the WFP to appeal to the government to grant permission for airdrops in

---

10 Cross-line areas are those areas that are reached by crossing hostile territories, such as bringing supplies from government-ruled territories into opposition-controlled areas.

the other 17 or 18 areas it besieged, and where 80 percent of the total besieged population in the country lives in dire conditions. Four months after it started air drops to the pro-government areas of Deir al-Zour, the WFP had still not been given permission by the government to make air drops in these other areas.[11]

The UN bureaucracy, probably for political expediency, prefers to use sanitized diplomatic language, blaming "parties" of the conflict for hampering access, when in reality blame can rarely be equally apportioned. The UN knows that with the exception of four areas (Kafraya, Fuaa, Nobbol, and al-Zahraa), it is the government which has been responsible for the rest of the 18 to 46 effectively besieged communities.[12] By controlling permits and denying access to humanitarian shipments or free movement to civilians, the government is effectively using food as a weapon. The Syrian government has more often than not denied the humanitarian agencies approval to work in certain locations, including the three besieged areas of Duma, East Harasta, and Darayya, which are "mere minutes" drive away from UN warehouses in Damascus, and where "some people are forced to eat grass to subsist."[13] Not that other actors did not do the same thing. The militias that besieged Fuaa and Kafraya in Idelb province did just the same. But the government is by far the biggest violator of international humanitarian law. In addition to rejecting requests on the pretext of security conditions, the Syrian government used the explicit threat of removing the UN's permission to operate within Syria and withdrawing visas for its non-Syrian staff members to keep humanitarians from delivering aid to Daraa. The Syrian government has used this threat consistently since then to manipulate where, how, and to whom the UN has been able to deliver humanitarian aid (Syria Campaign 2016:4). The Syrian government permissions could even be rescinded by government troops on the ground, as happened with an aid convoy to Darayya, in rural Damascus, on May 12, 2016: the last army checkpoint before the village denied

---

11 "WFP to Pursue Damascus Permission for Air Drops in Syria," Associated Press, June 3, 2016. Available at http://www.businessinsider.com/ap-wfp-to-pursue-damascus-permission-for-air-drops-in-syria-2016-6
12 For an updated map of besieged areas, see http://siegewatch.org/#7/35.111/38.540.
13 UN News Center 2016, quoting Stephen O'Brien, Under–Secretary General for Humanitarian Affairs and Emergency Relief Coordinator.

passage, stating that the convoy should not transport "medical items and baby milk." The UN secretary general complained that "conditions imposed by government security personnel are excessive and contrary to earlier guarantees and approvals obtained from the Government" (UN Secretary General 2016:9).

On June 14, 2016, a full four weeks after a formal request by the UN to send aid to 1.1 million people in 34 locations, the government refused access to a third of those people in areas it besieges or controls and agreed to partial delivery in another third of these locations (UN Secretary General 2016:11). Credible Syrian NGOs allege that diversion took place in favor of Syrian military and pro-government merchants in Deir al-Zour (Syria Institute and PAX 2016:36).

Besieging civilian areas in Syria is a flagrant violation of international humanitarian law and of four consecutive and relevant Security Council resolutions.[14] The uneven food aid delivery, including the biased airdrops to government areas, threatens to make the WFP's assistance effectively a part of the Syrian government's war strategy.

Where Islamic State and Kurds Have Control

The dynamics are markedly different in territories controlled by the forces of the Islamic State or the Kurds. Other organizations opted not to work in areas controlled by the Kurdish Democratic Union Party (whose Kurdish acronym is PYD), fearing a backlash from the Turkish government, as the PYD is allied with the Kurdistan Workers Party (PKK), which has long waged a violent campaign against the Turkish government.

In 2015, Kurdish fighters in Sheikh Maksoud in Aleppo were accused by a credible NGO of seizing a food shipment. The Kurdish group denied responsibility, but the NGO nonetheless avoided working in this area for two months until they were reassured the incident would not happen again. One organization, operating from across the Turkish border in Gaziantep to feed about 100,000 people a month, decided to work only in areas that are away from cross-lines and that have been stable for a predetermined period of time.

Almost all aid organizations opted not to work in ISIS-controlled areas after they rejected the radical and violent group's attempts in 2014

---

14 Resolutions 2139 (2014), 2165 (2014), 2191 (2014), and 2258 (2015) can all be accessed at http://www.un.org/en/sc/documents/resolutions/.

and 2015 to control their operations. Ceasing work in al-Raqqah province, most of Deir al-Zour province, and certain areas in northern rural Aleppo and elsewhere because of "their inability to work independently" (UN Secretary General 2016:10) stands in stark contrast to the way in which many of these same agencies continue to operate in the areas controlled by the Syrian government, albeit with a heavy dose of interference. These interventions at times included the removal of certain supplies, such as anesthetic drugs and other medicines, from aid trucks that were approaching their destinations in government-besieged areas. It is doubtful that it was only concerns about independence and impartiality that motivated the WFP not to work in ISIS areas.

Most aid organizations, in fact, avoid ISIS areas, fearing draconian US and European regulations about ensuring that no aid falls into the hands of terrorists.[15] One NGO director confirmed that they use international NGOs' access to lists of terrorist organizations and individuals suspected of terrorism to vet job candidates and companies that they might work with. This is not necessarily a foolproof method, simply because these lists are not the result of a credible process and people have gotten on and off them for spurious reasons. As one NGO director confirmed to me, "A supplier may have links to terrorist organizations or pay them money to get the stuff through, but we do not know this and we do not want to know it."

One UN aid worker scoffed at the question about the reasons for not operating in ISIS-controlled areas: "Ask the donors." Donors claim that aid agencies pulled out from ISIS-controlled areas because the extremist group wanted to control operations, but in essence this attempt at control is not radically different from what the Damascus government has been doing for years. One medical aid worker said they had to fold operations in ISIS-controlled areas after the Islamists' health ministry insisted on controlling the budget and salaries for medical workers. One aid worker whose organization ceased to operate in ISIS areas in early 2014 claimed ISIS demanded 25 to 30 percent cuts of all aid resources brought into their areas. He stressed that the politicization of aid is a twofold issue: militias like ISIS trying to control aid to gain credibility, and international NGOs and donors frantically questioning the respondent's organization constantly to make sure their work is not

---

15 Interviews with several aid workers in Gaziantep, April 2016.

benefiting ISIS in any way—even by making conditions for civilians living under their control more tolerable.[16] Organizations working in non–government controlled territories usually begin work after reaching agreements with local councils and security assurances, which are typically obtained through these councils from the dominant militias in the area. They sometimes transfer the risk to local trucking companies.

As one aid worker summed it up: every side "wants political gains out of aid operations." This complex situation (veiled and not-so-veiled security threats, donors' conditionality, and manipulation and threats from militias and the government) pushes organizations who work in ISIS-controlled or in Kurdish areas to either withdraw or keep a very low profile, which is at odds with their need for publicity and fundraising. Working in these areas also involves huge risks to the lives and safety of aid workers.

On the other hand, NGOs that are operating in the north cannot break the siege imposed by various militias on pro-government areas. One NGO manager summarily dismissed the possibility of working there.

These besieging groups which provide security assurances for our work in all other areas under their control would label us as traitors if we only dare to raise the possibility of providing for these . . . [pro-government] *villages. . . . If I dare take a convoy there, it means Jibhat al-Nusra would bar my organization from working in any area under their control.*[17]

Another aid worker pointed out that his organization was challenged by its own staff members, who did not want to help Shabiha or pro-government paramilitary thugs in Kafraya and Fuaa.[18]

According to one seasoned Syrian medical aid manager, humanitarian organizations have had to face security threats; negotiate with armed militias, the government, and local councils; and grapple with donor restrictions on where and with whom they can operate in Syria since 2012.

---

16 Interviews in Gaziantep, April 19, 2016.
17 Interviews with an NGO manager in Gaziantep, April 18, 2016.
18 Interview with an NGO manager in Gaziantep, April 19, 2016.

> *In every operation I have 15 various parties to worry about as both donors and militias question aid workers on the ground why they are assisting one side or the other and would not let them provide assistance easily to enemy groups or the other camp.*[19]

Food as a Weapon

What is the result of this government policy and these militia tactics, with which aid agencies on the ground are often forced to play along? Access to basic necessities, most importantly food, becomes severely limited and exorbitantly expensive, especially in government-besieged areas. Traders and smugglers also exploit the situation all the time. A few kilometers away from Damascus, the average food prices are many times more expensive than in the capital, whose army and allied militias impose the siege. According to the WFP's regular vulnerability assessment maps:

> *In May, Darayya continued to record the highest cost for a standard food basket: SYP 575,700—5.6 percent higher than in April and over twenty times the cost in Damascus. . . . In Madamiyet Elsham, fresh bread is only available when it could be smuggled in, costing more than SYP 1600/bundle (32 times higher than in Damascus). This price has increased by 13 percent since April and by 71 percent compared with six months ago.* (WFP VAM 2016:5–6)

In this way, the aid operations inadvertently turn the government-controlled areas into the only relatively viable governing order capable of ruling the country, while undermining the opposition-controlled areas. This disregards the principles of impartiality and neutrality by which the aid agencies are supposed to work. This unwilling collusion of the aid agencies is taking place because the third pillar of their work, independence, has been severely compromised.

The Dilemma of Aid Managers?

Setting aside higher politics and manipulation by big donors and Security Council permanent members, how do middle-level aid managers on the ground reach and justify their everyday decisions? Their logic is simple and betrays the fact that aid workers on the ground are aware of

---
19 Interview in Gaziantep, April 19, 2016.

the intricacies of instrumentalization and join the game of manipulation in a pragmatic way more often than not. They do not necessarily do this out of expediency and opportunism; sometimes it seems to be the best way to help as many needy people as possible and to save lives, regardless of the damaging medium- to long-term effects or harmful, even if unintended, consequences.

Syrian aid managers interviewed for this chapter argued that the government controlled the majority of the population in need and that this government can, as it has abundantly proven, curtail access. The field managers and their superiors in New York, Geneva, and Rome are then faced with the tough choice of whether to stand fast and refuse to be manipulated for political ends but risk jeopardizing aid shipments to hundreds of thousands of people in areas under government control. Without government permission to access besieged areas, the safety of shipments and aid workers will be at grave risk, they say. In its own evaluation of operations in Syria, the WFP management there said: "As a United Nations agency, WFP's role in delivering food to the maximum number of people in need was best served by maintaining relations with the Syrian Government and negotiating access" (Drummond et al. 2015:viii).

What aid managers have done is, in their opinion, the best under the circumstances, even if it unintentionally allows the Syrian government to use food aid as a weapon. This 'pragmatic' UN approach was rejected by over a hundred Syrian doctors and aid workers who sent a scathing letter to the UN humanitarian coordinator on January 13, 2016. They concluded:

> *For many of us in Syria, the UN has turned from a symbol of hope into a symbol of complicity. Two decades ago, in Srebrenica, we saw what happens when UN peacekeepers get dictated to by war criminals. Today in Syria, it seems to be the turn of UN humanitarians.*[20]

The Case of Iraq: From Convergence to Subservience

The WFP started preparing for a war in Iraq in late 2002, months before Washington launched it. When the massive humanitarian operation took place in the spring of 2003, the WFP consumed 75 percent of the total humanitarian resources for this year.

---

20 https://drive.google.com/file/d/0B4TiJ54YuM0qeHFZWHFfYTI1cUZzZGREbkd6VmZXNjhPSXY4/view

The Case of Iraq: From Convergence to Subservience

Only two years earlier, in 2001, the WFP had worked closely with the US government to coordinate with the US-led military on a massive aid operation in Afghanistan. Many humanitarian aid agencies in Afghanistan had worked closely with the U.S.-led coalition through the Provincial Reconstruction Teams, which comprised military forces working with civilians, including private contractors, to implement humanitarian and development aid operations (Walker and Maxwell 2008:75).

Like the massive WFP undertaking in Afghanistan, the Iraq operation was also largely funded by the US through USAID and by the UK through DfID (Department for International Development).[21] The Iraq operation, even more than the Afghanistan one, was a culmination of what British secretary of state for international development Clare Short described in 1997 as the 'New Humanitarianism,' which "recognized that all aid is political and that some of the ideals of the classical humanitarianism were a little old fashioned (none more so than the cherished classical ideal of neutrality)" (Walker and Maxwell 2008:73). In 2001, US Secretary of State Colin Powell called the humanitarian operations by US NGOs in Afghanistan a "force multiplier" in the fight against terrorism. These NGOs were under political and legal pressure to ensure continued funding from western donors that were involved in the war on terror. The independence of these NGOs became severely undermined in the process (Walker and Maxwell 2008:74).

Humanitarian aid to Iraq in 2003 totaled US $2 billion, 85 percent of which came from the US, the UK, and unobligated funds for the Security Council's Oil for Food (OFF) program that the Security Council decided to allocate to the humanitarian operation (UN OCHA Financial Tracking Services, n.d.). About 75 percent of all this money simply went to food aid—over US $1.5 billion—while protection and human rights received 0.2 percent, or US $4.7 million. The sheer size of the Iraq appeal and the massive media campaigns by aid agencies to raise funds (to make the operation look more multilateral rather than merely funded by the aggressors) lost these agencies even more credibility, especially in a region

---

21 As a WFP staff member in both operations I was privy to several meetings and exchanges with the two organizations. USAID kept an office for its staff within the WFP's office for a while in Islamabad. All donor figures for the WFP can be accessed at www.wfp.org.

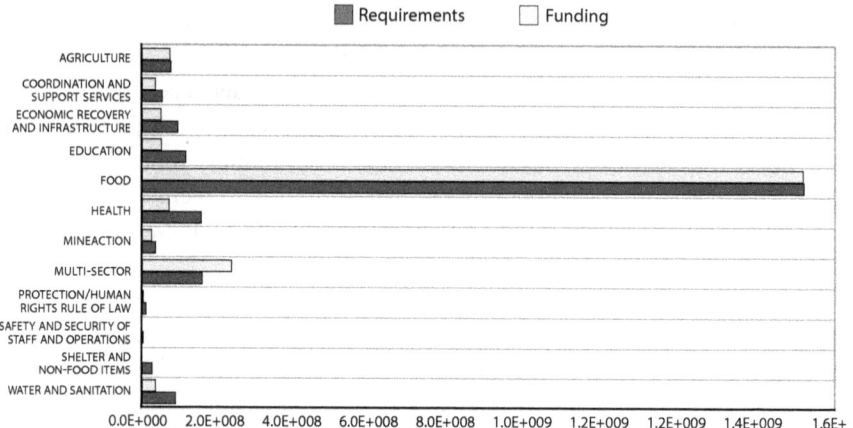

NOTE: *"Funding" means Contributions + Commitments*

Pledge: a non-binding announcement of an intended contribution or allocation by the donor. ("Uncommitted pledge" on these tables indicates the balance of original pledges not yet committed.)

Commitment: creation of a legal, contractual obligation between the donor and recipient entity, specifying the amount to be contributed.

Contribution: the actual payment of funds or transfer of in-kind goods from the donor to the recipient entity.

Figure 2. Consolidated appeal: Iraq crisis 2003. Requirements, contributions, and pledges by sector
(Source: UN OCHA Financial Tracking Services, as of February 7, 2017, at https://ftsarchive.unocha.org/reports/daily/ocha_R3sum_A605___19_January_2017_(02_30).pdf)

that had always viewed Iraq as a rich country thrown into poverty, not only because of the follies of its leaders, but even more because of the US-led sanctions and blockade since 1991.

The WFP involvement in Iraq goes back to the mid 1990s with the establishment of the Oil for Food (OFF) program, under which Iraq, suffering from the devastating impact of five years of draconian sanctions after it invaded Kuwait in 1990, was allowed to sell a certain amount of its oil production to procure basic humanitarian supplies, including food and medicine, under UN supervision.[22] The WFP was responsible for food distribution on behalf of the government of Iraq

---

22 The official UN information on the OFF can be accessed at https://www.un.org/depts/oip/background/index.html.

in the three semi-autonomous, predominantly Kurdish northern provinces through a chain of some 11,000 food agents, while WFP staff members observed the government distribution of food in the center and south through some 44,358 food agents. The role of the nearly 40 WFP observers was to provide data on the movement of commodities from warehouses and silos to beneficiaries and information on household food security.[23]

When the war became almost certain in the winter of 2002–2003, especially after Washington started negotiations within the Security Council in a failed attempt to obtain international legitimacy for invading Iraq to dismantle its alleged arsenal of weapons of mass destruction, aid agencies approached the U.S.-led coalition in contingency meetings through diplomatic channels to plan the humanitarian response. One of the leading humanitarian aid agencies operating in Iraq prepared a US $800 million contingency plan and shared it with the US administration.[24]

A few days after the US invasion on March 20, 2003, the first food commodities procured by the WFP arrived in Iraq. The first distributions of wheat flour started in April. In May, the distributions included rations of wheat flour, rice, pulses, oil, and detergents. The WFP was simply reproducing the monthly rations the government used to distribute.[25]

The WFP's role in the OFF program gave many Iraqis the impression that the UN humanitarian observers were responsible for the sanctions as well as for the occasional poor quality of the food rations, about which they regularly complained. These grievances ignored the facts that it was the Iraqi government that procured the food, and that the sanctions were imposed by the Security Council. The general public, justifiably, does not differentiate between the political and the humanitarian arms of the UN, while the WFP observers have never publicly pointed out the low food quality. The WFP agreed to play this OFF role

---

23 The WFP issued regular reports on its work in Iraq under the OFF program. The information in this paragraph comes from a 1997 report which can be accessed at http://reliefweb.int/report/iraq/wfp-emergency-report-no-23-1997-iraq.

24 Two separate UN officials confirmed to me that the WFP proposal was shared with the US government. The plan was shelved after objections within the WFP senior management team out of concern for appearing publicly as a part of the overall US strategy.

25 Regular WFP reports during the 1990s and 2000s, including 2003, can be found at http://www.un.org/Depts/oip/sector-food.html.

for operational interests and to maintain good relations with its largest donors (the US contributed more than half of WFP resources in the 1990s). The WFP operation in Iraq also created a lot of jobs and earned the organization a handsome overhead charge. The WFP teams withdrew just before the bombing started in March 2003, and then returned in April after the intense military operations were over to closely cooperate with the invading powers, without even bothering to explain to Iraqis the circumstances and the reasons for their withdrawal and the purpose of their redeployment.[26] This raised more suspicions about their allegiance and cast doubts on their neutrality and independence.

Before the US invasion it was difficult but not impossible to communicate with the Iraqi people through the BBC Radio's Arabic Service or the increasingly available regional Arab TV stations such as Al Jazeera, but UN agencies never really bothered to seriously invest in such efforts. After the invasion, it was even easier to communicate with the Iraqi people as local media platforms mushroomed. But the UN communication plans systematically ignored local audiences or relegated them to a very low priority. Of the four spokespersons who were active on behalf of UN humanitarian agencies (OCHA, WFP, UNICEF, and UNHCR), I was the only one who spoke Arabic, and I was often under pressure from headquarters to pay more attention to the international media for fundraising purposes or to send messages back to major donors or political allies in the west.

The US invasion of Iraq was not sanctioned by the UN, and it was seen as illegitimate by many Iraqis and Arabs in the wider region. The 'short leash' on which various aid agencies were held by donor governments who were party to the conflict were obvious to regional observers (Donini, Minear, and Walker 2004:192).

The WFP's work in Iraq under the OFF program, especially after the US invasion, could not unequivocally be categorized as a principled humanitarian undertaking. Even before the full disintegration of the Saddam regime in April 2003, the WFP had started plans to become the procurement and logistics consultant to the occupying power, the US-dominated Coalition Provisional Authority, to ensure the continuation of the massive public distribution system and avoid widespread

---

26 Most of the information in this section is gleaned from conversations with WFP colleagues in the early 2000s.

public discontent. This cast a long shadow on the alleged humanitarian nature of the WFP's work. There was practically no humanitarian crisis in large parts of the country. Even if the agency had not been there, there could have been some hardship but a for-profit contractor could probably have done most of the job. This 'fictional' humanitarianism was motivated by the WFP's operational and political priorities, but it exposed the widening gap between its work and the humanitarian principles of neutrality and independence even further.[27]

Humanitarian assistance in Iraq became a "central tenet of the hearts and minds component of current western counter-insurgency warfare doctrine. . . . It presents both an opportunity and a risk for humanitarians—it has led to vastly bigger budgets for humanitarian work but the money comes at a high risk to the independence and credibility of the agency that accepts it" (Walker and Maxwell 2008:75).

Depoliticized Professionalism

In 2003, the WFP had amazing logisticians and planners, who were able to move half a million tons of food from overseas and distribute them throughout Iraq every month. However, it lacked any nuanced reading of their context: the dominant local perceptions, the expectations, and the fast-shifting political sands. Such a reading would not have necessarily prevented terrorist attacks, but it might have permitted better decision making on communications, security, and programming. An aid worker needs technical expertise (nutrition, logistics, etc.), but also needs to be part anthropologist, economist, and security specialist, and to understand the local context culturally, linguistically, and above all, politically. But such well-rounded, informed, and knowledgeable aid workers do not come in abundance—to state it mildly. Technical professionalism is indispensable for the humanitarian effort but never sufficient. Ignoring other skills and the local knowledge can be worse than counterproductive.

Political compliance, donor pressure, organizational inertia, and the obsession about growth all contributed to the instrumentalization of the WFP's operation in Iraq. Aid agencies often do things because they have done them before the same way or because it would

---

[27] For a thorough discussion of UN agencies implicated in the Iraq operation, see Donini, Minear, and Walker (2004).

help grow their budgets and footprint. "The budget of single agencies began to rival the entire global spending on humanitarian action a mere decade or two earlier and in many cases exceed the annual budgets of many least developed countries" (Walker and Maxwell 2008:73). The WFP raised US $1.7 billion in 2000, US $1.9 billion in 2001 (the year of its Afghanistan operation), and US $3.6 billion in 2003 (the year of the Iraq operation; in this year over 40 percent of the WFP budget went to Iraq).[28] This means the organization doubled its size in only three years. It took another 12 years for WFP to almost double its budget again.

Conclusion

The consequences of aid politicization can be approached from two different perspectives. It can be seen as a blessing, whereby governments are integrating more humanitarian concerns into their foreign policies, culminating with the principle of humanitarian intervention or the Responsibility to Protect, as was the case with Libya in 2011 and the Balkans in the 1990s. On the other hand, politicization can lead to extreme instrumentalization, as we have seen in the cases of Iraq, Afghanistan, and now Syria.

Instrumentalization of food aid, and of aid operations in general, is in fact an old phenomenon.

> *Manipulation is in the DNA of humanitarian action. Politicization and manipulation go with the territory. . . . Humanitarian assistance has prolonged wars (Biafra) and provided a lifeline for genocidal or abusive regimes (Cambodia, North Korea); from Afghanistan to Zimbabwe, by way of Vietnam, Central America and Somalia, it has been used as a tool to advance Western agendas, as a band-aid to contain festering (political) sores, as a way of "doing something" other than handwringing or looking the other way. . . . Aid actors themselves have not been immune from using their presence and power to advance their own (or their sponsors') political agendas or to jostle for position and funds in the increasingly competitive political economy of the humanitarian enterprise.* (Donini 2012:246)

---

28 WFP annual reports can be found at http://www.wfp.org/policy-resources/corporate?type=38&tid_2=all&tid_4=all.

Conclusion

There has never been a golden age for humanitarianism. States are not the only ventriloquists. In the late 1980s, the UNHCR started to lose support and funding, entering the 1990s with people questioning its very existence. Then UNHCR chief Sadako Ogata said that the organization "should not give up on a project just because it does not fit into traditional schemes. . . . In order to be financed in a highly competitive environment, UNHCR must develop new, interesting approaches to fulfill its core mandate" (Barnett 2011:208). And this indeed took place as the UNHCR started to work on preventive and in-country protection under pressure from countries that no longer wanted to receive refugees. This was a gigantic change for an organization whose mandate had previously been to care for refugees once they crossed borders, not to help them when they were displaced within their own country. But by moving to work inside countries in which people were fleeing the persecution of authorities or militias, the UNHCR often had to work with these very authorities, or at least gain their permission. It also had to start working on other aspects of prevention, including human rights, democratization, and even market stabilization in terms of program planning. The WFP's trajectory is not much different.

Aid work has always been politicized to one degree or another, if we take this to mean the influence of factors beyond the narrowly defined needs of the assisted, but this politicization has deepened and broadened since the end of the Cold War as governments increasingly and selectively embraced human rights and humanitarian intervention as part of the driving principles of their foreign policy. This provides the humanitarian industry with opportunities to influence decisions that would have been impossible in the past, such as the intervention in Libya in 2011, but also puts them at the mercy of much larger powers that can use them in wars of choice, such as the invasion of Iraq in 2003 or the Syrian civil war since 2012.

> *Such humanitarianism, tagged along with western strategy, or playing along with one or more parties to the conflict will lose credibility in those parts of the world where the west is least impartial and will be seen as a tool of western interests and culture. . . . Aid will become a tool of self interest.* (Vaux 2001:204)

This is a very fitting description of what happened in Iraq in 2003 and is being repeated in Syria, notwithstanding the exaggerated focus on the west. Figure 1 shows the complexity and multiple interactions among all relevant actors, each of which is part of the processes of manipulation.

This chapter has shown that instrumentalization was not crudely imposed on the WFP, but sometimes actively sought by the organization for the purpose of institutional preservation. This is why, over the past 20 years, in complex ways and forms, the organization has moved away from general food distribution for the needy, now only used in the early phase of an emergency, into using food as a tool for 'development,' especially in protracted emergency situations. Food for work, food for education, food for training, and food for asset creation all became fashionable interventions to make the WPF look like an organization that is interested in the root causes of conflict and in intervening to address them, rather than only dealing with the symptoms. But this apparently simple move ultimately means also entering the political fray in full force and adopting positions on governance, political reform, reconstruction, and peacebuilding. This means the WFP and other organizations that have taken a similar route had to be involved in programs such as disarmament, demobilization and reintegration of militias, return of refugees and displaced people, recovery of decimated communities, rebuilding basic agricultural infrastructure, supporting land reform, and many other thoroughly political endeavors. More often than not, they would have to take sides in complex issues where donors, recipient governments, and affected communities never have one and the same view. Taking sides in such issues is much more a political than a technical decision.

The UN's credibility as a humanitarian actor has suffered a series of grievous blows since the early 1990s, and specifically in Somalia. But it continued to bleed and become less and less impartial from then on. Bosnia (1991–1995), Rwanda (1994), Kosovo (1996–1998), and Afghanistan (2001) are all stark cases of the evolution of the integration of humanitarian aid into political and military plans. This increasing integration was carried out by both design and interest by all parties involved, including a majority of aid agencies.

Iraq in 2003 is blatant case of the integration of humanitarian action into the political plans of a warring party to ensure stability in the transition period, while Syria is the ultimate case in which the aid actors,

Conclusion

especially on the food-aid front, have become effectively integrated in the military strategies of the regime as well as its external opponents (primarily the US and other western donors). The beneficiaries themselves and the local opposition militias occupy an insignificant position at the decision-making table. In both cases, institutional preservation and maintaining a seat at the table with the big boys were major drivers for some aid agencies. From that perspective, it was always more important to see to donors' needs and maintain a relationship with the governments and authorities on the ground rather than stick to the humanitarian principles of impartiality, neutrality, and independence.

In order to properly analyze the humanitarian enterprise, we must always look at its multiple, crisscrossing relationships with the liberal states, dominant market forces, and rule-of-law institutions (Barnett 2011:162). This also means looking at donors (largely northern and western), corporations, local non-governmental organizations, recipient states and communities, and aid bureaucracies. This viewpoint will help us understand how humanitarian actors are influenced, by what tools, under what pressures, and how they and other actors from other quarters all take part in the instrumentalization of humanitarian aid.

A major barrier between humanitarian actors and political instrumentalization cracked and then fell down in the 1990s due to major global political and economic shifts. Relief or emergency aid was reconstrued as part of a continuum on which peacebuilding, peacekeeping, conflict prevention, human rights, democratization, and emergency aid coexist and must harmonize their efforts. This forced aid actors to pay attention to highly political considerations, especially those of their donors and regulators, as they designed and implemented their relief programs.

Humanitarianism is made up of "ethics and politics, of solidarity and diversity, of emancipation and domination," and its history reflects "much about the changing global order in which we live" (Barnett 2011:18). What is happening in Syria now is yet another example of the articulation of power politics and humanitarian aid in such a way that the effort has sometimes hurt the very people it is meant to help.

Despite all of these trends, instrumentalization is not an inexorable force. A large number of aid workers, researchers, media, and members of the vulnerable groups themselves are now far more aware of the politics of humanitarian aid, thanks to more established transparency projects (the Sphere Project and the Humanitarian Accountability Partnership are good examples). The disclosure of information by donors to the media and to receiving communities, the increasing scrutiny from the media, and the access of vulnerable groups to social media all reinforce this trend. These innovations, brought about by several humanitarian actors who are well aware of the shortcomings of the systems and the pitfalls of wild politicization and integration, are probably the main hope for a progressive reform of the humanitarian aid system. Even when new normative frameworks for humanitarian aid do not decrease the instrumentalization, they document and expose it.

As Barnett hoped, humanitarians and all those involved in this gigantic system would indeed learn their lessons well if the ensuing evaluation reports, new codes of conduct, and impact assessment lead to new systems of accountability (Barnett 2011:217). This will happen when aid workers and agencies more openly defend humanitarian principles in their own right and not because they would serve this or that political agenda; when the recipients exercise more leverage; when financing systems become less western-dominated; and when influential donors are more effectively firewalled from governance in the aid system. There is no certainty that these developments will take place soon, but there are enough signs to indicate that humanitarianism as we know it now is not sustainable.

References

Barnett, M. 2011. *Empire of Humanity: A History of Humanitarianism.* Ithaca and London: Cornell University Press.

Donini, A., ed. 2012. *The Golden Fleece: Manipulation and Independence in Humanitarian Action.* Sterling, VA: Kumarian Press.

Donini, A., L. Minear, and P. Walker. 2004. "The Future of Humanitarian Action: Mapping the Implications of Iraq and Other Recent Crises," *Disasters*, 26: 190–204.

Donini, A., and P. Walker. 2012. "So What." In A. Donini, ed. *The Golden Fleece: Manipulation and Independence in Humanitarian Action*, 243–263. Sterling, VA: Kumarian Press.

Drummond, J., et al. 2015. "An Evaluation of WFP's Regional Response to the Syrian Crisis, 2011–2014." WPF Office of Evaluation, OEV/2014/19. http://documents.wfp.org/stellent/groups/public/documents/reports/wfp274337.pdf

Sida, L., L. Trombetta, and V. Panero. 2016. *Evaluation of OCHA Response to the Syria Crisis*. New York: United Nations Office for the Coordination of Humanitarian Affairs. https://docs.unocha.org/sites/dms/Documents/OCHA%20Syria%20Evaluation%20Report_FINAL.pdf

Syria Campaign. 2016. *Taking Sides: The United Nations' Loss of Impartiality, Independence and Neutrality in Syria*. The Syria Campaign. http://takingsides.thesyriacampaign.org/wp-content/uploads/2016/06/taking-sides.pdf

Syria Institute and PAX. 2016. *Siege Watch: Second Quarterly Report on Besieged Areas in Syria, May 2016*. http://siegewatch.org/wp-content/uploads/2015/10/PAX_TSI_REPORT_Syria_Siege_FINALweb.pdf

UN News Centre. 2016. "Grim Conditions in Syria Despite Greater Access." http://www.un.org/apps/news/story.asp?NewsID=53575#.VvzwvhJ9637

UN OCHA Financial Tracking Services. N.d. "Iraqi Crisis 2003." http://fts.unocha.org/pageloader.aspx?page=emerg-emergencyDetails&appealID=605

UN Secretary General. 2016. *Implementation of Security Council Resolutions 2139 (2014), 2165 (2014), 2191 (2014) and 2258 (2015): Report of the Secretary-General*. http://www.un.org/en/ga/search/view_doc.asp?symbol=S/2016/546

Vaux, T. 2001. *The Selfish Altruist: Relief Work in Famine and War*. London: Earthscan.

Walker, P., and D. Maxwell. 2008. *Shaping the Humanitarian World*. London: Routledge.

Walker, P., and S. Purdin. 2004. "Birthing Sphere," *Disaster*, 28:2: 100–111.

WFP (World Food Programme). 2016. *Year in Review 2015*. Rome: WFP. http://documents.wfp.org/stellent/groups/public/documents/communications/wfp284681.pdf

WFP (World Food Programme) VAM. 2016. *Syria: Food Insecurity Remains High as Prices Increase*. Bulletin, June 4. http://documents.wfp.org/stellent/groups/public/documents/ena/wfp284843.pdf

About the Contributors

Dr. Habib Ayeb is a geographer at Université Paris 8.

Hala N. Barakat is a freelance environmentalist and food researcher.

Dr. Iman Hamdy is the editor of Cairo Papers in Social Science.

Christian Handerson is a PhD candidate, Development Studies Department, School of Oriental and African Studies.

Dr. Ellis Goldberg is emeritus professor of political science, University of Washington.

Dr. Saker El Nour is a postdoctoral researcher, School of Advanced Social Science Studies (EHESS) and the Museum of European and Mediterranean Civilizations (MuCEM), France.

Khaled Mansour is an independent writer and consultant.

Sara Pozzi is a PhD candidate in social anthropology, School of Social Science, University of Manchester.

Sara El Sayed is a co-founder of Nawaya.

Dr. Malak Rouchdy is assistant professor of sociology, the American University in Cairo.

CAIRO PAPERS IN SOCIAL SCIENCE

Volume One, 1977–1978
1   *Women, Health and Development*, Cynthia Nelson, ed.
2   *Democracy in Egypt*, Ali E. Hillal Dessouki, ed.
3   *Mass Communications and the October War*, Olfat Hassan Agha
4   *Rural Resettlement in Egypt*, Helmy Tadros
5   *Saudi Arabian Bedouin*, Saad E. Ibrahim and Donald P. Cole

Volume Two, 1978–1979
1   *Coping With Poverty in a Cairo Community*, Andrea B. Rugh
2   *Modernization of Labor in the Arab Gulf*, Enid Hill
3   *Studies in Egyptian Political Economy*, Herbert M. Thompson
4   *Law and Social Change in Contemporary Egypt*, Cynthia Nelson and Klaus Friedrich Koch, eds.
5   *The Brain Drain in Egypt*, Saneya Saleh

Volume Three, 1979–1980
1   *Party and Peasant in Syria*, Raymond Hinnebusch
2   *Child Development in Egypt*, Nicholas V. Ciaccio
3   *Living Without Water*, Asaad Nadim et al.
4   *Export of Egyptian School Teachers*, Suzanne A. Messiha
5   *Population and Urbanization in Morocco*, Saad E. Ibrahim

Volume Four, 1980–1981
1   *Cairo's Nubian Families*, Peter Geiser
2, 3   *Symposium on Social Research for Development: Proceedings*, Social Research Center
4   *Women and Work in the Arab World*, Earl L. Sullivan and Karima Korayem

Volume Five, 1982
1   *Ghagar of Sett Guiranha: A Study of a Gypsy Community in Egypt*, Nabil Sobhi Hanna
2   *Distribution of Disposal Income and the Impact of Eliminating Food Subsidies in Egypt*, Karima Korayem
3   *Income Distribution and Basic Needs in Urban Egypt*, Amr Mohie el-Din

Volume Six, 1983
1. *The Political Economy of Revolutionary Iran*, Mihssen Kadhim
2. *Urban Research Strategies in Egypt*, Richard A. Lobban, ed.
3. *Non-alignment in a Changing World*, Mohammed el-Sayed Selim, ed.
4. *The Nationalization of Arabic and Islamic Education in Egypt: Dar al-Alum and al-Azhar*, Lois A. Arioan

Volume Seven, 1984
1. *Social Security and the Family in Egypt*, Helmi Tadros
2. *Basic Needs, Inflation and the Poor of Egypt*, Myrette el-Sokkary
3. *The Impact of Development Assistance On Egypt*, Earl L. Sullivan, ed.
4. *Irrigation and Society in Rural Egypt*, Sohair Mehanna, Richard Huntington, and Rachad Antonius

Volume Eight, 1985
1, 2 *Analytic Index of Survey Research in Egypt*, Madiha el-Safty, Monte Palmer, and Mark Kennedy

Volume Nine, 1986
1. *Philosophy, Ethics and Virtuous Rule*, Charles E. Butterworth
2. *The 'Jihad': An Islamic Alternative in Egypt*, Nemat Guenena
3. *The Institutionalization of Palestinian Identity in Egypt*, Maha A. Dajani
4. *Social Identity and Class in a Cairo Neighborhood*, Nadia A. Taher

Volume Ten, 1987
1. *Al-Sanhuri and Islamic Law*, Enid Hill
2. *Gone For Good*, Ralph Sell
3. *The Changing Image of Women in Rural Egypt*, Mona Abaza
4. *Informal Communities in Cairo: the Basis of a Typology*, Linda Oldham, Haguer el Hadidi, and Hussein Tamaa

Volume Eleven, 1988
1. *Participation and Community in Egyptian New Lands: The Case of South Tahrir*, Nicholas Hopkins et al.
2. *Palestinian Universities Under Occupation*, Antony T. Sullivan
3. *Legislating Infitah: Investment, Foreign Trade and Currency Laws*, Khaled M. Fahmy
4. *Social History of An Agrarian Reform Community in Egypt*, Reem Saad

Volume Twelve, 1989
1   *Cairo's Leap Forward: People, Households, and Dwelling Space*, Fredric Shorter
2   *Women, Water, and Sanitation: Household Water Use in Two Egyptian Villages*, Samiha el-Katsha et al.
3   *Palestinian Labor in a Dependent Economy: Women Workers in the West Bank Clothing Industry*, Randa Siniora
4   *The Oil Question in Egyptian-Israeli Relations, 1967–1979: A Study in International Law and Resource Politics*, Karim Wissa

Volume Thirteen, 1990
1   *Squatter Markets in Cairo*, Helmi R. Tadros, Mohamed Feteeha, and Allen Hibbard
2   *The Sub-culture of Hashish Users in Egypt: A Descriptive Analytic Study*, Nashaat Hassan Hussein
3   *Social Background and Bureaucratic Behavior in Egypt*, Earl L. Sullivan, el Sayed Yassin, Ali Leila, and Monte Palmer
4   *Privatization: the Egyptian Debate*, Mostafa Kamel el-Sayyid

Volume Fourteen, 1991
1   *Perspectives on the Gulf Crisis*, Dan Tschirgi and Bassam Tibi
2   *Experience and Expression: Life Among Bedouin Women in South Sinai*, Deborah Wickering
3   *Impact of Temporary International Migration on Rural Egypt*, Atef Hanna Nada
4   *Informal Sector in Egypt*, Nicholas S. Hopkins, ed.

Volume Fifteen, 1992
1   *Scenes of Schooling: Inside a Girls' School in Cairo*, Linda Herrera
2   *Urban Refugees: Ethiopians and Eritreans in Cairo*, Dereck Cooper
3   *Investors and Workers in the Western Desert of Egypt: An Exploratory Survey*, Naeim Sherbiny, Donald Cole, and Nadia Makary
4   *Environmental Challenges in Egypt and the World*, Nicholas S. Hopkins, ed.

Volume Sixteen, 1993
1. *The Socialist Labor Party: A Case Study of a Contemporary Egyptian Opposition Party*, Hanaa Fikry Singer
2. *The Empowerment of Women: Water and Sanitation Initiatives in Rural Egypt*, Samiha el Katsha and Susan Watts
3. *The Economics and Politics of Structural Adjustment in Egypt: Third Annual Symposium*
4. *Experiments in Community Development in a Zabbaleen Settlement*, Marie Assaad and Nadra Garas

Volume Seventeen, 1994
1. *Democratization in Rural Egypt: A Study of the Village Local Popular Council*, Hanan Hamdy Radwan
2. *Farmers and Merchants: Background for Structural Adjustment in Egypt*, Sohair Mehanna, Nicholas S. Hopkins, and Bahgat Abdelmaksoud
3. *Human Rights: Egypt and the Arab World, Fourth Annual Symposium*
4. *Environmental Threats in Egypt: Perceptions and Actions*, Salwa S. Gomaa, ed.

Volume Eighteen, 1995
1. *Social Policy in the Arab World*, Jacqueline Ismael and Tareq Y. Ismael
2. *Workers, Trade Union and the State in Egypt: 1984–1989*, Omar el-Shafie
3. *The Development of Social Science in Egypt: Economics, History and Sociology; Fifth Annual Symposium*
4. *Structural Adjustment, Stabilization Policies and the Poor in Egypt*, Karima Korayem

Volume Nineteen, 1996
1. *Nilopolitics: A Hydrological Regime, 1870–1990*, Mohamed Hatem el-Atawy
2. *Images of the Other: Europe and the Muslim World Before 1700*, David R. Blanks et al.
3. *Grass Roots Participation in the Development of Egypt*, Saad Eddin Ibrahim et al.
4. *The Zabbalin Community of Muqattam*, Elena Volpi and Doaa Abdel Motaal

Volume Twenty, 1997
1. *Class, Family, and Power in an Egyptian Village*, Samer el-Karanshawy
2. *The Middle East and Development in a Changing World*, Donald Heisel, ed.
3. *Arab Regional Women's Studies Workshop*, Cynthia Nelson and Soraya Altorki, eds.
4. *"Just a Gaze": Female Clientele of Diet Clinics in Cairo: An Ethnomedical Study*, Iman Farid Bassyouny

Volume Twenty-one, 1998
1   *Turkish Foreign Policy During the Gulf War of 1990–1991*, Mostafa Aydin
2   *State and Industrial Capitalism in Egypt*, Samer Soliman
3   *Twenty Years of Development in Egypt (1977–1997): Part I*, Mark C. Kennedy
4   *Twenty Years of Development in Egypt (1977–1997): Part II*, Mark C. Kennedy

Volume Twenty-two, 1999
1   *Poverty and Poverty Alleviation Strategies in Egypt*, Ragui Assaad and Malak Rouchdy
2   *Between Field and Text: Emerging Voices in Egyptian Social Science*, Seteney Shami and Linda Hererra, eds.
3   *Masters of the Trade: Crafts and Craftspeople in Cairo, 1750–1850*, Pascale Ghazaleh
4   *Discourses in Contemporary Egypt: Politics and Social Issues*, Enid Hill, ed.

Volume Twenty-three, 2000
1   *Fiscal Policy Measures in Egypt: Public Debt and Food Subsidy*, Gouda Abdel-Khalek and Karima Korayem
2   *New Frontiers in the Social History of the Middle East*, Enid Hill, ed.
3   *Egyptian Encounters*, Jason Thompson, ed.
4   *Women's Perception of Environmental Change in Egypt*, Eman el Ramly

Volume Twenty-four, 2001
1, 2   *The New Arab Family*, Nicholas S. Hopkins, ed.
3   *An Investigation of the Phenomenon of Polygyny in Rural Egypt*, Laila S. Shahd
4   *The Terms of Empowerment: Islamic Women Activists in Egypt*, Sherine Hafez

Volume Twenty-five, 2002
1, 2   *Elections in the Middle East: What Do They Mean?* Iman A. Hamdy, ed.
3   *Employment Crisis of Female Graduates in Egypt: An Ethnographic Account*, Ghada F. Barsoum
4   *Palestinian and Israeli Nationalism: Identity Politics and Education in Jerusalem*, Evan S. Weiss

Volume Twenty-six, 2003
1   *Culture and Natural Environment: Ancient and Modern Middle Eastern Texts*, Sharif S. Elmusa, ed.
2   *Street Children in Egypt: Group Dynamics and Subcultural Constituents*, Nashaat Hussein

3 *IMF–Egyptian Debt Negotiations*, Bessma Momani
4 *Forced Migrants and Host Societies in Egypt and Sudan*, Fabienne Le Houérou

Volume Twenty-seven, 2004
1, 2 *Cultural Dynamics in Contemporary Egypt*, Maha Abdelrahman, Iman A. Hamdy, Malak Rouchdy, and Reem Saad, eds.
3 The Role of Local Councils in Empowerment and Poverty Reduction, Solava Ibrahim
4 *Beach Politics: Gender and Sexuality in Dahab*, Mustafa Abdalla

Volume Twenty-eight, 2005
1 *Creating Families Across Boundaries: A Case Study of Romanian/Egyptian Mixed Marriages*, Ana Vinea
2, 3 *Pioneering Feminist Anthropology in Egypt: Selected Writings from Cynthia Nelson*, Martina Rieker, ed.
4 *Roses in Salty Soil: Women and Depression in Egypt Today*, Dalia A. Mostafa

Volume Twenty-nine, 2006
1 *Crossing Borders, Shifting Boundaries: Palestinian Dilemmas*, Sari Hanafi, ed.
2, 3 *Political and Social Protest in Egypt*, Nicholas S. Hopkins, ed.
4 *The Experience of Protest: Masculinity and Agency among Sudanese Refugees in Cairo*, Martin T. Rowe

Volume Thirty, 2007
1 *Child Protection Policies in Egypt: A Rights-Based Approach*, Adel Azer, Sohair Mehanna, Mulki Al-Sharmani, and Essam Ali
2 *"The Farthest Place": Social Boundaries in an Egyptian Desert Community*, Joseph Viscomi
3 *The New York Egyptians: Voyages and Dreams*, Yasmine M. Ahmed
4 *The Burden of Resources: Oil and Water in the Gulf and the Nile Basin*, Sharif S. Elmusa, ed.

Volume Thirty-one, 2008
1 *Humanist Perspectives on Sacred Space*, David Blanks, Bradley S. Clough, eds.
2 *Law as a Tool for Empowering Women within Marital Relations: A Case Study of Paternity Lawsuits in Egypt*, Hind Ahmed Zaki
3,4 *Visual Productions of Knowledge: Toward a Different Middle East*, Hanan Sabea, Mark R. Westmoreland, eds.

Volume Thirty-two, 2009
1   *Planning Egypt's New Settlements: The Politics of Spatial Inequities,* Dalia Wahdan
2   *Agrarian Transformation in the Arab World: Persistent and Emerging Challenges,* Habib Ayeb and Reem Saad
3   *Femininity and Dance in Egypt: Embodiment and Meaning in al-Raqs al-Baladi,* Noha Roushdy
4   *Negotiating Space: The Evolution of the Egyptian Street, 2000–2011,* Dimitris Soudias

Volume Thirty-three, 2010
1   *Masculinities in Egypt and the Arab World: Historical, Literary, and Social Science Perspectives,* Helen Rizzo, ed.
2   *Anthropology in Egypt 1900–1967: Culture, Function, and Reform,* Nicholas S. Hopkins
3   *The Church in the Square: Negotiations of Religion and Revolution at an Evangelical Church in Cairo,* Anna Jeannine Dowell

Volume Thirty-four
1   *Egyptian Hip-Hop: Expressions From the Underground,* Ellen R. Weis
2   *Sports and Society in the Middle East,* Nicholas S. Hopkins and Sandrine Gamblin, eds.
3   *Organizing the Unorganized: Migrant Domestic Workers in Lebanon,* Farah Kobaissy

www.ingramcontent.com/pod-product-compliance
Lightning Source LLC
Chambersburg PA
CBHW070800040426
42333CB00060B/1723